*Here's what people are saying about
the DOING LIFE TOGETHER Series . . .*

Small Group Members Are Saying...

Six weeks ago we were strangers. Today we are a family in Christ. We talk to each other, lean on each other, encourage each other, and hold each other accountable. We have gone from meeting as a Bible study to getting together for several social events, meeting for Sunday services, and organizing service projects in our community.

—Sandy and Craig

The Purpose-Driven material quickly moved us beyond group and closer toward family, beyond reading God's Word to knowing God!

—The Coopers

Small Group Leaders Are Saying...

Even though our group has been together for several years, the questions in this study have allowed us to connect on a much deeper level. Many of the men are displaying emotions we haven't seen before.

—Steve and Jennifer

The material has become a personal compass to me. When I find myself needing to make a decision, I ask, "Does it bring me closer to God's family? Does it make me more like Christ? Am I using the gifts God gave me? Am I sharing God's love? Am I surrendering my life to please God?" I still have a long way to go, but this has been a blessing and a compass to keep me on his path.

—Craig

Pastors and Church Leaders Are Saying...

We took the entire church through this curriculum, and the results were nothing less than miraculous. Our congregation was ignited with passion for God and his purposes for our lives. It warmed up the entire congregation as we grew closer to God by "Doing Life Together."

—Kerry

The Purpose-Driven format helped our groups realize there are some areas that they are doing very well in (fellowship and discipleship) and other areas that they need to do some work in. What is amazing is to see how they are committing to work on these areas (especially evangelism and ministry).

—Steve

Other Studies in the DOING LIFE TOGETHER Series

Beginning Life Together (God's Purposes for Your Life)

Connecting with God's Family (Fellowship)

Growing to Be Like Christ (Discipleship)

Sharing Your Life Mission Every Day (Evangelism)

Surrendering Your Life for God's Pleasure (Worship)

After you complete this study, we'd love to hear how DOING LIFE TOGETHER has affected your life, your group, or your church! Write us at stories@lifetogether.com. You can also log on to www.lifetogether.com to see how others are putting "life together" into practice.

life**together** ^{DOING}

DEVELOPING YOUR
SHAPE TO SERVE OTHERS

six sessions on
ministry

written by
BRETT and **DEE EASTMAN**
TODD and **DENISE WENDORFF**
KAREN LEE-THORP

ZONDERVAN™

GRAND RAPIDS, MICHIGAN 49530 USA

ZONDERVAN™

Developing Your SHAPE to Serve Others
Copyright © 2002 by Brett and Deanna Eastman, Todd and Denise Wendorff,
and Karen Lee-Thorp

Requests for information should be addressed to:

Zondervan, *Grand Rapids, Michigan 49530*

ISBN 0-310-24675-X

Interior icons by Tom Clark

Printed in the United States of America

---

04 05 06 07 08 09 10 /❖ DC/ 19 18 17 16

CONTENTS

Foreword   7
Acknowledgments   9
Read Me First   11

SESSION 1   You Are God's Masterpiece   15
SESSION 2   A Servant's Heart   22
SESSION 3   Discovering Your Gifts   30
SESSION 4   Your Unique Personality   39
SESSION 5   Serving from Experience   47
SESSION 6   Serving with Your Whole Heart   56

FREQUENTLY ASKED QUESTIONS   64

APPENDIX
            Purpose-Driven Group Agreement   67
            Small Group Calendar   69
            Purpose Team Roles   70
            Purpose-Driven Life Health Assessment   72
            Purpose-Driven Life Health Plan   74
            Spiritual Partners' Check-In Page   77
            SHAPE Worksheet   78
            Memory Verses   80
            Daily Devotional Readings   81
            Prayer and Praise Report   82
            Sample Journal Page   84

LEADERSHIP TRAINING
            Small Group Leadership 101   85
                (Top Ten Ideas for New Facilitators)
            Small Group Leadership Lifters   88
                (Weekly Leadership Tips)
            Leader's Notes   93

About the Authors   107
Small Group Roster   108

FOREWORD

Over twenty-five years ago I noticed a little phrase in Acts 13:36 that forever altered the direction of my life. It read, *"David had served God's purpose in his own generation."* I was fascinated by that simple yet profound summary of David's life, and I determined to make it the goal of my life, too. I would seek to discover and fulfill the purposes for which God had created me.

This decision provoked a number of questions: What are God's purposes for putting us on earth? What does a purpose-driven life look like? How can the church enable people to fulfill God's eternal purposes? I read through the Bible again and again, searching for the answers to these questions. As a direct result of what I learned, my wife, Kay, and I decided to start Saddleback Church and build it from the ground up on God's five purposes for us (which are found in the New Testament).

In the living laboratory of Saddleback Church, we were able to experiment with different ways to help people understand, apply, and live out the purposes of God. I've written two books about the lessons we've learned (*The Purpose-Driven Church* and, more recently, *The Purpose-Driven Life*). As other churches became interested in what we were doing, we began sharing the tools, programs, and studies we developed at Saddleback. Over a million copies of *The Purpose-Driven Church* are now in print in some nineteen languages, and The Purpose-Driven Class Curriculum (Class 101–401) is now used in tens of thousands of churches around the world. We hope that the same will be true for this exciting new small group curriculum.

DOING LIFE TOGETHER is a groundbreaking study in several ways. It is the first small group curriculum built completely on the purpose-driven paradigm. This is not just another study to be used *in* your church; it is a study *on* the church to help *strengthen* your church. Many small group curricula today are quite self-focused and individualistic. They generally do not address the importance of the local church and our role in it as believers. Another unique feature of this curriculum is its balance. In every session, the five purposes of God are stressed in some way.

But the greatest reason I am excited about releasing this DOING LIFE TOGETHER curriculum is that I've seen the dramatic changes it produces in the lives of those who study it. These small group studies were not developed in some detached ivory tower or academic setting but in the day-to-day ministry of Saddleback Church, where thousands of people meet weekly in small groups that are committed to fulfilling God's purposes. This curriculum has been tested and retested, and the results have been absolutely amazing. Lives have been changed, marriages saved, and families strengthened. And our church has grown—in the past seven years we've seen over 9,100 new believers baptized at Saddleback. I attribute these results to the fact that so many of our members are serious about living healthy, balanced, purpose-driven lives.

It is with great joy and expectation that I introduce this resource to you. I am so proud of our development team on this project: Brett and Dee Eastman, Todd and Denise Wendorff, and Karen Lee-Thorp. They have committed hundreds of hours to write, teach, develop, and refine these lessons —with much feedback along the way. This has been a labor of love, as they have shared our dream of helping you serve God's purpose in your own generation. The church will be enriched for eternity as a result.

Get ready for a life-changing journey. God bless!

—Pastor Rick Warren

Pastor Rick Warren is the author of *The Purpose-Driven Church* and *The Purpose-Driven Life* [www.purposedrivenlife.com].

ACKNOWLEDGMENTS

Sometimes in life God gives you a dream. Most of the time it remains only a dream. But every once in a while, a dream captures your heart, consumes your thoughts, and compels you to action. However, if others around you aren't motivated to share the dream and aren't moved to action along with you, it remains just that—a dream. By the grace of God and a clear call on the hearts of a few, our dream has become a reality.

The DOING LIFE TOGETHER series was birthed one summer in the hearts of Brett and Dee Eastman and Todd and Denise Wendorff, two Saddleback Church staff couples. They hoped to launch a new one-year Bible study based on the Purpose-Driven® life. They called it *The Journey: Experiencing the Transformed Life. The Journey* was launched with a leadership team that committed its heart and soul to the project. We will never be able to express our gratitude to each of you who shared the dream and helped to continue the dream now, three years later.

Early on, Karen Lee-Thorp, an experienced writer of many Bible studies, joined the team. Oh, God, you are good to us!

Saddleback pastors and staff members too numerous to mention have supported our dream and have come alongside to fan the flames. We would have never gotten this off the ground without their belief and support.

We also want to express our overwhelming gratitude to the numerous ministries and churches that helped shape our spiritual heritage. We're particularly grateful for Bill Bright of Campus Crusade for Christ, who gave us a dream for reaching the world, and for Bill Hybels of Willow Creek Community Church, who gave us a great love and respect for the local church.

Our special thanks goes to Pastor Rick and Kay Warren for sharing the dream of a healthy and balanced purpose-driven church that produces purpose-driven lives over time. It clearly is the basis for the body of this work. God only knows how special you are to us and how blessed we feel to be a part of your team.

Finally, we thank our beloved families who have lived with us, laughed at us, and loved us through it all. We love doing our lives together with you.

READ ME FIRST
DOING LIFE TOGETHER

DOING LIFE TOGETHER is unique in that it was designed in community for community. Four of us have been doing life together, in one way or another, for over fifteen years. We have been in a small group together, done ministry together, and been deeply involved in each other's lives. We have shared singleness, marriage, childbirth, family loss, physical ailments, teenage years, job loss, and, yes, even marital problems.

Our community has not been perfect, but it has been real. We have made each other laugh beyond belief, cry to the point of exhaustion, feel as grateful as one can imagine, and get so mad we couldn't see straight. We've said things we will always regret and shared moments we will never forget, but through it all we have discovered a diamond in the rough—a community that increasingly reflects the character of Jesus Christ. God has used our relationships with each other to deepen our understanding of and intimacy with him. We have come to believe that we cannot fully experience the breadth and depth of the purpose-driven life outside of loving relationships in the family of God (Ephesians 2:19–22; 4:11–13).

Doing life together was God's plan from the beginning of time. From the relationships of Father, Son, and Holy Spirit in the Trinity, to the twelve apostles, to the early house churches, and even Jesus' final words in the Great Commission (Matthew 28:16–20)—all share the pattern of life together. God longs to connect all of his children in loving relationships that cultivate the five biblical purposes of the church deep within their hearts. With this goal in mind, we have created the DOING LIFE TOGETHER series—the first purpose-driven small group series.

The series is designed to walk you and your group down a path, six weeks at a time over the course of a year, to help you do the purpose-driven life together. There are six study guides in this series. You can study them individually, or you can follow the one-year path through the six studies. *Beginning Life Together* offers a six-week overview of the purpose-driven life. The other five guides (*Connecting with God's Family, Growing to Be Like Christ, Developing Your SHAPE to Serve Others, Sharing Your Life Mission Every Day,* and *Surrendering Your Life for God's Pleasure*) each explore one of the five purposes of the church more deeply.

In his book *The Purpose-Driven Life*, Rick Warren invites you to commit to live a purpose-driven life every day. The DOING LIFE TOGETHER series was designed to help you live this purpose-driven life through being part of a purpose-driven small group. A purpose-driven group doesn't simply connect people in community or grow people through Bible study. These groups seek to help each member balance all five biblical purposes of the church. The fivefold purpose of a healthy group parallels the fivefold purpose of the church.

Designed for Service

When a medieval craftsman wanted to prove himself worthy of the rank of master, he set about creating a piece that would display his full artistry. He poured all of his skill and passion into it, for it was his duty to shape common materials into a supreme example of his craft. If his guild accepted it, this work was called his *masterpiece*.

You are God's masterpiece. He created you to express his genius. You express it in who you are when you're not doing anything, yet you're not just a museum piece. You were made to do things only you can do. God has equipped you with spiritual gifts, abilities, experiences, temperament, and a heart like no one else's. You are irreplaceable.

The world needs you to offer all of who you are in service to God. If you're sitting on the sidelines of life and watching others serve, the world is diminished. If you're struggling under a burden of tasks you were never designed for, the world isn't benefiting from the heart you could offer if you only had the time. God longs to see your service well up from a joyful heart that knows what it was made for. It's time to start being who you were born to be.

There are several ways to discover and develop your unique design. One is through self-assessments such as the SHAPE process described in this guide. Another is by getting feedback from others, as you'll do several times in this study. A third and crucial way is to experiment with areas of service. You'll have a chance to do that as well. Bible study and prayer will find their fruit in action.

Outline of Each Session

Most people desire to live a purpose-driven life, but few people actually achieve this on a consistent basis. That's why we've included elements of the five purposes in every meeting—so that you can live a healthy, balanced spiritual life over time.

When you see the following symbols in this book, you will know that the questions and exercises in that section promote that particular purpose.

 CONNECTING WITH GOD'S FAMILY (FELLOWSHIP). The foundation for spiritual growth is an intimate connection with God and his family. The questions in this section will help you get to know the members of your small group so that you'll begin to feel a sense of belonging. This section is designed to open your time together and provide a fun way to share your personal stories with one another.

 GROWING TO BE LIKE CHRIST (DISCIPLESHIP). This is the most exciting portion of each lesson. Each week you'll study one or two core passages from the Bible. The focus will be on how the truths from God's Word make a difference in your lives. We will often provide an experiential exercise to enable you not just to talk about the truth but also to experience it in a practical way.

 DEVELOPING YOUR SHAPE TO SERVE OTHERS (MINISTRY). Most people want to know how God has uniquely shaped them for ministry and where they can serve in the center of his will. This section will help make that desire a reality. Every week you will be encouraged to take practical steps in developing who God uniquely made you to be in order to serve him and others better.

 SHARING YOUR LIFE MISSION EVERY DAY (EVANGELISM). Many people skip over this aspect of the Christian life because it's scary, relationally awkward, or simply too much work for their busy schedules. We understand, because we have these thoughts as well. But God calls all of us to reach out a hand to people who don't know him. It's much easier to take practical, manageable steps that can be integrated naturally into everyday life if you take them together.

 SURRENDERING YOUR LIFE FOR GOD'S PLEASURE (WORSHIP). A surrendered heart is what pleases God most. Each small group session will give you a chance to surrender your heart to God and one another in prayer. In addition, you'll be introduced to several forms of small group worship, including listening to worship CDs, singing together, reading psalms, and participating in Communion. This portion of your meeting will transform your life in ways you never thought possible. If you're new to praying in a small group, you won't be pressed to pray aloud until you feel ready.

STUDY NOTES. This section provides background notes on the Bible passage(s) you examine in the GROWING section. You may want to refer to these notes during your study.

FOR FURTHER STUDY. This section can help your more spiritually mature members take the session one step further each week on their own. If your group is ready for deeper study or is comfortable doing homework, this section and the following two sections will help you get there. You may want to encourage them to read these passages and reflect on them in a personal journal or in the Notes section at the end of each session.

MEMORY VERSES. For those group members who want to take a step of hiding God's Word in their hearts, there are six memory verses on page 80 that correspond to each weekly lesson. You may want to tear out this page and cut the verses into wallet- or purse-size cards for easy access.

PURPOSE-DRIVEN LIFE READING PLAN. This plan for reading *The Purpose-Driven Life* by Rick Warren parallels the weekly sessions in this study guide. *The Purpose-Driven Life* is the perfect complement to the DOING LIFE TOGETHER series. If your group wants to apply the material taught in the book, you can simply read the recommended piece each week, write a reflection, and discuss the teaching as a group or in pairs.

DAILY DEVOTIONS. One of the easiest ways for your group to grow together is to encourage each other to read God's Word on a regular basis. It's so much easier to stay motivated in this area if you have one another's support. On page 81 is a daily reading plan that parallels the study and helps you deepen your walk with God. There are five readings per week. If you really want to grow, we suggest you pair up with a friend (spiritual partner) to encourage each other throughout the week. Decide right now, and write the name of someone you'd like to join with for the next six weeks.

YOU ARE GOD'S MASTERPIECE

When I was in college, someone challenged me to go on a mission trip overseas. At first I said, "NO WAY! I am not qualified or interested." I had never known a missionary. What kind of person goes on mission trips? I had recently started growing in my relationship with the Lord and in no way saw myself as fit to represent God in the world. I didn't even think I was valuable enough to him to be used for his purposes.

I then came across the passage in Ephesians (2:10) that says we are God's masterpieces, created to do good works. I was amazed that even I—a wild woman who loved to have fun, lacked discipline, crammed for finals, and lived for UCLA football games—could be part of God's plans. I began to dream about what God might want to do in my life. What was his desire? How had he uniquely made me? I did end up going overseas, and God used me in ways I never dreamed possible. Even more, he convinced me that I was significant—even at that early stage in my journey.

—Denise

CONNECTING WITH GOD'S FAMILY   10 min.

1. God has uniquely designed each of us. Share with the group one positive quality that God has given you.

2. It's important for every group to agree on a set of shared values. If your group doesn't already have an agreement (sometimes called a covenant), turn to page 67. Even if you've been together for some time and your values are clear, the Purpose-Driven Group Agreement can help your group achieve greater health and balance. We recommend that you especially consider rotating group leadership, setting up spiritual partners,

and introducing purpose teams into the group. Simply go over the values and expectations listed in the agreement to be sure everyone in the group understands and accepts them. Make any necessary decisions about such issues as refreshments and child care.

GROWING TO BE LIKE CHRIST   20 min.

Have you ever thought about the distinctive qualities that God has woven together to make you uniquely you? Your fingerprints are one of a kind. All your physical attributes, your personality, the way you think, your experiences, your passions, your abilities, and even your failures make up the unique person you are. Nothing about you is a mistake. In Psalm 139 the psalmist expresses to God his astonishment about what God has done:

> *For you created my inmost being;*
> *you knit me together in my mother's womb.*
> *14I praise you because I am fearfully and wonderfully*
> *made;*
> *your works are wonderful,*
> *I know that full well.*
> *15My frame was not hidden from you*
> *when I was made in the secret place.*
> *When I was woven together in the depths of the earth,*
> *16   your eyes saw my unformed body.*
> *All the days ordained for me*
> *were written in your book*
> *before one of them came to be.*
> *—Psalm 139:13–16*

3. How do you respond to the idea that God has fearfully and wonderfully made you?

4. We often wonder if God is fully aware of certain parts of us, especially the parts we're not proud of. We compare ourselves to others, and wonder if God has made a mistake in creating us. What is one thing that's hard for you to accept about the way God has designed you?

   Maybe you feel you're no longer a masterpiece because sin has marred what God made. You've made sinful choices, and others have sinned against you. All this has left its mark on who you are now. In truth, you are a glorious ruin, a stained masterpiece. You may find it easier to see the stains than the masterpiece. You may think that the stains erase your value. But God calls you to change your focus. In love, God is using even the stains to restore the masterpiece to greater glory. Transformed by grace, even your faults and painful experiences are becoming part of your beauty.

5. "All the days ordained for me were written in your book." To what extent do you think God planned the childhood experiences that shaped you?

   How do you feel about God's hand in your childhood?

For it is by grace you have been saved, through faith—and this not from yourselves, it is the gift of God—⁹not by works, so that no one can boast. ¹⁰For we are God's workmanship, created in Christ Jesus to do good works, which God prepared in advance for us to do.

—Ephesians 2:8–10

6. You are God's workmanship, God's masterpiece. For what kinds of "good works" do you think God created you?

7. How do you feel about serving God as his workmanship or masterpiece here on earth?

8. God made each of you as a masterpiece and now pours out his grace to restore you to masterpiece condition. Pause for a moment to thank him for these things. Ask God to help you see past your flaws to the masterpiece he made you to be.

DEVELOPING YOUR SHAPE TO SERVE OTHERS   10 min.

If your group has been together for six weeks or more, you can probably see strengths in each other that they don't see in themselves.

9. Give each person an index card or a blank greeting card, and ask him or her to write his or her name on it. Then have everyone pass their card to the person on their right. This person will write on the card a word or phrase that describes a positive quality or ability the other has. Keep passing the cards to the right until each person has written on each card and the cards have made their way back to their owners. The cards will now list a number of positive qualities that the group sees in each person.

SURRENDERING YOUR LIFE FOR GOD'S PLEASURE   15–30 min.

Your good works need not be burdens. They are meant to flow out of your intimate connection with your Creator. Here are some ways you can strengthen that connection.

10. On page 81 you'll find a list of brief passages for daily devotions—five per week for the six weeks of this study. If you've never spent daily time with God, this is an easy way to begin. Would you consider taking on this habit for the duration of this study? See page 84 for a sample journal page that you can use as a guide for your daily devotions.

    If you're already consistent in daily devotions, consider acquiring the habit of Scripture memory. Six memory verses are provided on page 80—one verse per week. Would you consider accepting the challenge to memorize one verse per week and hide God's Word in your heart? We urge you to pair up with another person for encouragement and accountability.

11. In order to allow more prayer time for everyone, quickly gather into small circles of three or four people. Allow everyone to answer this question: "How can we pray for you this week?"

    Take some time to pray for these requests in your small circles. Ask God to show each of you a good work you were created to do this week. Anyone who isn't used to praying aloud should feel free to offer prayers in silence. Or, if you're new to prayer and you're feeling brave, try praying just one sentence: "Thank you, God, for. . . ." Be sure to have one person write down your requests and share them later with the group or leaders.

STUDY NOTES

Wonderfully made. In Hebrew, _pala'_—"to be distinct, marked out, to be separated, to be distinguished."* This passage declares that God uniquely designs each human being. It's up to us to discover this uniqueness and express it through our lives. The psalmist emphasizes this idea by repeating the same word in the next sentence ("[God's] works are _pala'_"). Extraordinary are we who have been created, the psalmist tells us.

For it is by grace you have been saved, through faith. This is one of the most important phrases in the Bible. It declares that we are saved from the consequences of our sins by God's unearned kindness, not because we deserve to be let off the hook. We receive this offer of unearned forgiveness by placing our faith or trust in Jesus Christ. Our faith rests not on what _we_ do to win salvation but on what _God_ has done in Jesus. Grace is a free gift. Service is a voluntary, eager response to grace. True service is the upwelling of a grateful heart that feels deeply loved, not the grudging duty of a heart that feels coerced.

Workmanship. _Poiēma_ in Greek—literally, "a work of art." (We get our word _poem_ from this word.) We are works of art, just like Michelangelo's _David_ or the Sistine Chapel. Notice that we are saved by grace for a purpose. We are each to live as full expressions of God's unique masterpiece.

Prepared ahead of time. God purposed ahead of time a unique way in which we would serve him, using our giftedness, our makeup, and even our negative experiences. See also Psalm 139:16, in which the Hebrew word _yatsar_ means "ordained ahead of time."

☐ **_For Further Study_** on this topic, read Genesis 1:27; Job 31:4; Matthew 6:26.

☐ **_Weekly Memory Verse:_** Psalm 139:14

☐ **_The Purpose-Driven Life Reading Plan:_** Day 29

---

* _"Pala'," The Online Bible: Thayer's Greek Lexicon and Brown Driver & Briggs Hebrew Lexicon,_ copyright ©1993, Woodside Bible Fellowship, Ontario, Canada. Licensed from the Institute for Creation Research.

If you're using the DVD along with this curriculum, please use this space to take notes on the teaching for this session.

A SERVANT'S HEART

I walked into the men's rest room between Sunday services and passed a man in a wheelchair at the wash counter. He had a tube of toothpaste out, his shirt was off, and he was attempting to wash up. I concluded that he was homeless. Fear struck me: "God, are you going to ask me to help him?" I didn't know if I could do anything for him. I wrestled with God and finally washed up next to the man and left.

As I walked out, I felt a stab of guilt. I should have asked him if he needed help. *This lonely man*, I thought, *probably doesn't have a friend in the world*. It occurred to me that, although I struggled with the thought of reaching out and loving this man, if I had only seen him through Jesus' eyes, I would have seen him so differently. Jesus would have taken the time to bring spiritual healing into his life through some act of love. Jesus' heart always inclined toward serving others and loving them, regardless of the cost.

—Todd

CONNECTING WITH GOD'S FAMILY   10 min.

1. Think of someone who has served you—someone who has gone out of his or her way to respond to a need in your life. How did he or she serve you? How did you feel?

GROWING TO BE LIKE CHRIST   30–40 min.

A servant's heart doesn't come naturally to any of us. The willingness to set aside our own agendas is essential for learning how God wants us to use our abilities. Jesus shows us the way:

Jesus called them together and said, "You know that those who are regarded as rulers of the Gentiles lord it over them, and their high officials exercise authority over them. ⁴³Not so with you. Instead, whoever wants to become great among you must be your servant, ⁴⁴and whoever wants to be first must be slave of all. ⁴⁵For even the Son of Man did not come to be served, but to serve, and to give his life as a ransom for many."

—Mark 10:42–45

2. In the world you live in, what does it take to be "great" (significant, respected, valued)?

3. According to Jesus, what does it take to be "great" in God's kingdom?

4. How do the "great" behave in the world? In God's kingdom?

Jesus showed with his life what he meant by serving. The apostle Paul explained:

If you have any encouragement from being united with Christ, if any comfort from his love, if any fellowship with the Spirit, if any tenderness and compassion, ²then make my joy complete by being like-minded, having the same love, being one in spirit and purpose. ³Do nothing out of selfish ambition or vain conceit, but in humility consider others better than yourselves. ⁴Each of you should look not only to your own interests, but also to the interests of others.

⁵Your attitude should be the same as that of Christ Jesus:

⁶Who, being in very nature God,
did not consider equality with God something to be
grasped,
⁷but made himself nothing,
taking the very nature of a servant,
being made in human likeness.
⁸And being found in appearance as a man,
he humbled himself
and became obedient to death—even death on a cross!
                                        —Philippians 2:1–8

5. What did it cost Jesus to serve you (verses 6–8)?

6. How did Paul describe the servant's attitude in verses 2–4 above?

7. "Consider others better than yourselves" (verse 3). Does this mean you should have a low self-image and act like a doormat? Explain your thoughts.

8. Where in your life do you feel the tension between seeking greatness in people's eyes and seeking greatness in God's eyes? Or the tension between serving your own interests and serving others' interests?

9. God calls us to serve even people who don't seem to deserve it. Who is one such person in your life?

10. Pause to pray that God will empower you to live with a servant's heart in the situations you've described. Pray for each member of the group.

DEVELOPING YOUR SHAPE TO SERVE OTHERS   15–20 min.

11. How do you develop a servant's heart? One helpful step is to take a look at the current state of your heart. The Purpose-Driven Life Health Assessment on page 72 is a tool to help you identify the state of your heart in various areas. Take a few minutes right now to rate yourself in the DEVELOPING section of the assessment. You won't have to share your scores with the group.

12. Pair up with your partner from last week or someone in the group with whom you feel comfortable discussing your assessment. We recommend that men partner with men and women with women. Groups of three are also fine. Talk about these three questions:

- **What's hot?** (In what ways are you doing well?)
- **What's not?** (In which areas do you need the most growth?)
- **What's next?** (What is one goal that you think God would like you to work on over the next thirty days? What will you do to reach that goal?)

Here are examples of possible goals:

☐ At least three days a week I will pray for God to give me the kind of servant's heart that Jesus had.
☐ At least three days a week I will use a journal to write about that day's struggle with pride and humility.

☐ I will help lead my group in a service project that we will begin within the next four weeks.

☐ I will volunteer to help with a particular area of service at my church. That area is

_____

_____.

☐ I will check in with _____ at least once a week to let him or her know how I'm doing at living out of a servant's heart.

Your ultimate aim may be a change in attitude: "I want to become more humble and willing to serve." But becoming more humble is vague enough that you might be tempted to let it slide. It will be more helpful to choose a consistent action that will help you grow in humility, such as focused prayer, confession, journaling, accountability, or practice in service. The action is not an end in itself but a tool to help you notice and begin to shift your heart attitudes.

Write your goal here:

The person you've paired up with can be your spiritual partner to support you in reaching your goal. In two of the next four group sessions you will briefly check in with your spiritual partner about your personal progress. You can also call or send an E-mail to each other between meetings.

If you've never taken the Purpose-Driven Life Health Assessment, consider rating yourself in the remaining four areas this week.

13. As you worked through question 10, you spent some time in prayer. Close now in prayer briefly with your spiritual partner(s). You can share any prayer requests that haven't already come up. Pray especially for the Spirit's power to fulfill the plans you have made. If you're new to praying aloud, it's okay to pray silently or to pray by using just one sentence: "God, please help _____ to

_____."

As you leave, remember

- your goal for the next thirty days.
- to keep on with your daily devotions.
- to hide God's Word in your heart through your weekly Scripture memory verse.

STUDY NOTES

Lord it over. To take advantage of others for your own benefit or to try to bring them under your control.

Serve. The same Greek word can mean "serve" or "minister." When we serve others, we are ministers.

Slave. Jesus' language here is shockingly drastic. A slave is considered another person's property. Slaves did the lowliest work in Roman times. It isn't likely that Jesus means we should act as though other people own us; in fact, God owns us. (In 1 Corinthians 6:19–20, Paul says that God bought us at the cost of his Son's life. But he bought us to be free servants.) More likely, Jesus means we should freely choose the kind of lowly service that proud people would leave for slaves to do. Jesus is not advising us to let others dominate and control us. (Jesus himself served constantly but never let others control him.) We need a strong awareness of our true Master if we want to choose lowly service without being controlled by people.

Humility. Modesty in how we view ourselves. We view ourselves as insufficient but God as extremely sufficient. We are nothing without God's power and strength, but because we have God's strength, we don't need to prove we are something. Life for the humble person is not a self-image roller coaster ride from highs ("Look at me; I'm Somebody!") to lows ("Man, what a jerk; I'm Nobody"). The humble person doesn't think much about his or her self-image, because it's a settled issue.

Consider others better than yourselves. This doesn't mean we look down on ourselves or view ourselves as less significant than others. Rather, when we are willing to take on the mind-set of a servant, we see another's needs as more important than our own.

Taking the very nature of a servant. In becoming human, Jesus was a servant to mankind. His frame of thinking was to serve others, not himself.

☐ *For Further Study* on this topic, read John 13:1–20; Matthew 11:7–19; Romans 12:9–21.

☐ *Weekly Memory Verse:* Mark 10:43

☐ *The Purpose-Driven Life Reading Plan:* Days 30–31

_____

_____

_____

_____

_____

_____

_____

_____

_____

_____

_____

_____

_____

_____

_____

_____

_____

_____

_____

_____

_____

_____

_____

_____

_____

_____

_____

_____

_____

If you're using the DVD along
with this curriculum, please use
this space to take notes on the
teaching for this session.

DISCOVERING YOUR GIFTS

When I met Monica at the gym, I was amazed at her incredible leadership and at her ability to motivate others in the physical realm. She was a twenty-eight-year-old personal trainer with a unique ability to lead others to change and grow in the area of fitness. I invited her to join the class that Denise and I lead—a class that includes small group time and emphasizes personal time with God. Monica decided to give it a try. We leaders were more than glad to send love and encouragement her way. Late in the year we invited class members to share how their devotions were going. Monica stood and shared how much she was loving her time with God. Her enthusiasm wowed the group. We leaders could see her gift for leadership and communication, so we began to tell her that she could be a leader in the spiritual world the way she was in the fitness world. We asked her to speak to the whole class at our last meeting of the year, and once again she shone.

The following year Monica agreed to lead one of the small groups. People kept wanting to join her group, and she even invited friends from the gym. Her magnetic personality and leadership skills were drawing woman after woman into her group. Her experience with a group of loving people who helped her discern her gifts had transformed her into a committed disciple and an effective servant of Jesus Christ.

—Dee

CONNECTING WITH GOD'S FAMILY   10 min.

1. What is one word, image, or question that comes to your mind when you hear the term *spiritual gifts*? (Examples: *Mysterious. A preacher speaking to a large crowd. Can I have spiritual gifts and not know it?*)

GROWING TO BE LIKE CHRIST

Spiritual gifts were a source of competition and debate in the fledgling church in Corinth. Some people felt proud to have the "important" gifts, while others felt they had nothing to offer. These attitudes are still common today. But as Paul explains, not one of us has reason to be arrogant or embarrassed. God designs each of us differently to reflect the many parts of him.

There are different kinds of gifts, but the same Spirit. ⁵There are different kinds of service, but the same Lord. ⁶There are different kinds of working, but the same God works all of them in all men.

⁷Now to each one the manifestation of the Spirit is given for the common good. . . .

¹⁴Now the body is not made up of one part but of many. ¹⁵If the foot should say, "Because I am not a hand, I do not belong to the body," it would not for that reason cease to be part of the body. ¹⁶And if the ear should say, "Because I am not an eye, I do not belong to the body," it would not for that reason cease to be part of the body. ¹⁷If the whole body were an eye, where would the sense of hearing be? If the whole body were an ear, where would the sense of smell be? ¹⁸But in fact God has arranged the parts in the body, every one of them, just as he wanted them to be. ¹⁹If they were all one part, where would the body be? ²⁰As it is, there are many parts, but one body.

²¹The eye cannot say to the hand, "I don't need you!" And the head cannot say to the feet, "I don't need you!" ²²On the contrary, those parts of the body that seem to be weaker are indispensable, ²³and the parts that we think are less honorable we treat with special honor. And the parts that are unpresentable are treated with special modesty, ²⁴while our presentable parts need no special treatment. But God has combined the members of the body and has given greater honor to the parts that lacked it, ²⁵so that there should be no division in the body, but that its parts should have equal concern for each other. ²⁶If one part suffers, every part suffers with it; if one part is honored, every part rejoices with it.

—1 Corinthians 12:4–7, 14–26

2. Three times in verses 4–6 Paul repeats that all spiritual gifts and all acts of true service come from the same Spirit of God. Why do you suppose he makes such a big deal about this?

3. God gives spiritual gifts "for the common good" (verse 7). What kind of impact should this have on our understanding and practice of spiritual gifts?

4. Paul compares the Christian community to a human body. What can we learn about spiritual gifts from the way bodies function (verses 14–26)?

5. If all the gifts are equally important, why do we often feel we are less important and less useful?

DEVELOPING YOUR SHAPE TO SERVE OTHERS   30–40 min.

God has designed you to serve him in unique ways. Only you can contribute what you were made for. Spiritual gifts are one aspect of your uniqueness. They receive the most attention in the New Testament, because the Holy Spirit gives them only to people who put their faith in Jesus Christ. Unbelievers have unique skills, personalities, passions, and experiences that offer much to the world, but only believers have spiritual gifts. That's because a person has to yield his or her life to the Holy Spirit's leadership in order to receive the Holy Spirit's gifts.

Saddleback Valley Community Church uses a framework called SHAPE to help people think through how God has designed them. SHAPE stands for

- **S**piritual gifts
- **H**eart
- **A**bilities
- **P**ersonality
- **E**xperiences

In this session you will try to identify your spiritual gifts and natural abilities. In sessions 4, 5, and 6 you'll look at personality, experiences, and heart. At the end of the six weeks, you will have evaluated yourself in each area of SHAPE. You will then be able to discern a ministry for which you are uniquely suited.

The Bible does not lock us into tight restrictions with respect to the number of spiritual gifts, or even their definitions. The four major lists of gifts are found in Romans 12:3–8; 1 Corinthians 12:1–11, 27–31; Ephesians 4:11–12; and 1 Peter 4:9–11 (but there are other passages as well that mention or illustrate gifts not included in these lists). These are probably not meant to be exhaustive lists of all the possible gifts. God could gift you to do almost anything he wanted done! Every believer has at least one gift, and one person can have many gifts.

6. Take a few minutes on your own to read the list of gifts on pages 34–35. Place check marks next to the spiritual gifts you think you have or may have.

Gifts That Communicate God's Word

☐ Prophecy   1 Corinthians 14:3

The ability to publicly or personally communicate God's word regarding a specific situation with challenge, comfort, and conviction so as to point people toward Jesus Christ and his will

☐ Evangelism   Acts 8:26–40

The ability to communicate the good news about Jesus Christ easily and naturally to unbelievers so that they often respond with faith

☐ Missions   1 Corinthians 9:19–23; Acts 13:2–3

The ability and flexibility to bring Jesus to a culture or people other than your own

☐ Apostle   Romans 15:20

The ability to plant new churches and oversee their development

Gifts That Educate God's People

☐ Teaching   Ephesians 4:12–13

The ability to teach the Bible or train others in a way that causes them to learn and implement life-change

☐ Encouragement   Acts 14:22

(sometimes called Exhortation)

The ability to care for others in a way that builds their courage and motivates them to follow Jesus; the ability to bring out the best in others

☐ Wisdom   1 Corinthians 2:1, 6–16

The ability to understand God's perspective on life situations and share these insights in a simple, understandable way

☐ Discernment   1 Corinthians 2:14

The ability to know whether one is following the Spirit of God or the spirit of error in a given situation

Gifts That Demonstrate God's Love

☐ Service   Acts 6:1–7

The ability to give practical assistance in a way that makes people feel cared for and loved; the ability to see opportunities to serve without being asked

☐ Mercy   Romans 12:8

The ability to show practical compassion toward suffering persons; the ability to sense people's thoughts and emotions in order to care for them

☐ Hospitality   1 Peter 4:9–10
The ability to make strangers feel welcomed and comfortable

☐ Pastoring   1 Peter 5:2–4
(sometimes called Shepherding)
The ability to walk with others through life in a caring way that helps
them grow in faith; the ability to care for people's spiritual needs and
equip them for service. (This gift can be exercised in a small group, not
just in full-time ministry.)

☐ Giving   2 Corinthians 8:1–7
The ability to give of your resources without feeling put out

☐ Miracles   Mark 11:23–24
The ability to pray in faith for God's supernatural intervention into an
impossible situation and see God answer; the ability to sense when God
is prompting you to pray this kind of prayer

Gifts That Celebrate God's Presence (Worship- or Prayer-Related Gifts)

☐ Intercession   Colossians 1:9–12
The ability to pray persistently for others

☐ Healing   James 5:14–16
The ability to bring physical or emotional healing into another's life
through prayer

☐ Praying with My Spirit   1 Corinthians 14:13–15
(sometimes called Tongues/Interpretation)
The ability to pray in a language understood only by God or one
who interprets

☐ Music and Arts   Psalm 150
The ability to create art that elevates people into God's presence

Gifts That Support All Four Purposes

☐ Leadership   Hebrews 13:7–17
The ability to bring out the best in others in their service to God; the
ability to set vision, motivate, equip, train, or set an example of service
in order to draw a group to reach a goal

☐ Administration   1 Corinthians 14:40
(sometimes called Organization)
The ability to manage people well and organize programs and ministries
effectively

☐ Faith   Romans 4:18–21
The ability to trust God and to act on God's promise, regardless of what
the circumstances indicate; the willingness to risk failure in pursuit of a
God-given vision, expecting God to handle the obstacles

7. Now look at the SHAPE Worksheet on pages 78–79. Place check marks next to the *spiritual gifts* you marked above. Also place check marks next to the *abilities* you believe you have. Add to the list any of your abilities you don't see recorded there.

8. Ask for a volunteer to go first in a time of sharing. This person will share *one* gift or ability with the group. Allow others either to affirm the gifts they see or to suggest alternatives. Then have the next person share, and again have the group respond. Keep the discussion moving, so that everyone gets a chance to gain feedback about his or her gifts and abilities. Even if you've been together for only a short time, you may be surprised at the intuitions others have about your possible gifts.

 SURRENDERING YOUR LIFE FOR GOD'S PLEASURE   20 min.

9. Sit next to your spiritual partner(s). Together do one or more of the following:

    • Share what you learned from your devotional time this week.
    • Recite your memory verse.
    • Tell how you're doing with the goal you set for yourself.

10. Team up with another pair of spiritual partners to form a prayer circle. Share a brief prayer request. Have one person write down the requests. Then pray for each other, especially to discover and use your spiritual gifts. If you're new to praying aloud, try praying one sentence: "Lord, please _____ _____." If you prefer to pray silently, you can simply say "amen" to let the group know you're finished.

STUDY NOTES

Gifts. Endowments or empowerments given by the Spirit of God. People are born with some abilities and develop their skills through practice, but they receive spiritual gifts when the Holy Spirit bestows gifts. Once given, gifts usually need to be developed through practice.

Working. *Energēma*—we get our English word "energy" from this word. Our gifts in action work in others' lives with spiritual power.

Common good. Gifts are not given to puff us up or to win people's attention or respect. They are for the good of others—the good of the whole community.

Now the body is not made up of one part but of many. There are no insignificant body parts. Some parts are not as noticeable as others, but *all* are essential for the body's proper health.

☐ *For Further Study* on this topic, read Romans 12:1–8; 1 Peter 4:10–11; Ephesians 4:11–13.

☐ *Weekly Memory Verse:* 1 Peter 4:10

☐ *The Purpose-Driven Life Reading Plan:* Day 32

NOTES

If you're using the DVD along
with this curriculum, please use
this space to take notes on the
teaching for this session.

4 YOUR UNIQUE PERSONALITY

Some days I wish I were an extrovert. I wish I could walk into a huge roomful of strangers and enjoy meeting all of them. I take on speaking engagements from time to time, and while I love to teach, meeting the crowd of people before and afterwards wears me out. I feel awkward. I long to take just one person aside for an hour and really get to know him or her.

Most days I have an introvert's dream job. I write books. My husband goes to work, and I spend the whole day at home in my little office—alone. In the silence I have ideas, and my computer turns them into chapters, sentence by sentence. When I describe my job, extroverts shudder.

Writing books is one of the ways by which I serve God. A book can touch many hearts. So when I walk into a crowded room, I try to remember to say, "Thank you, God, that I'm weak in situations like this. I know you made me just the way you wanted."

—Karen

CONNECTING WITH GOD'S FAMILY   10 min.

Because we are all unique, we view life differently and have different preferences. Have fun noticing your differences as you answer question 1.

1. Describe your ideal vacation.

GROWING TO BE LIKE CHRIST   20 min.

One person's ideal vacation is an active romp through an unfamiliar city. Another's ideal is a quiet rest beside the ocean with a good book. God made us different! And as with the differences between eyes and ears, different is good.

Any given personality trait can be a strength or a weakness, depending on whether it has been surrendered to God and purified in the fire of the Holy Spirit. To see how God used one man's personality for God's glory, consider Paul. (For more background on Paul, see the study note on page 45 and the leader's notes on page 104.) Paul described himself like this:

> For you have heard of my previous way of life in Judaism, how intensely I persecuted the church of God and tried to destroy it. [14]I was advancing in Judaism beyond many Jews of my own age and was extremely zealous for the traditions of my fathers. [15]But when God, who set me apart from birth and called me by his grace, was pleased [16]to reveal his Son in me so that I might preach him among the Gentiles, I did not consult any man, [17]nor did I go up to Jerusalem to see those who were apostles before I was, but I went immediately into Arabia and later returned to Damascus.
>
> —Galatians 1:13–17

2. What can you learn about Paul's personality from this brief passage?

3. What traits did Paul have that could have been either positive or negative, depending on how well he surrendered them to God?

Paul became a leader of the Christian movement. He spent the rest of his life walking thousands of miles to take the good news about Jesus Christ throughout the Roman Empire, until eventually Paul was arrested and executed.

Mary of Bethany's personality was quite different:

> *Six days before the Passover, Jesus arrived at Bethany,*
> *where Lazarus lived, whom Jesus had raised from the dead.*
> *²Here a dinner was given in Jesus' honor. Martha served, while*
> *Lazarus was among those reclining at the table with him. ³Then*
> *Mary took about a pint of pure nard, an expensive perfume; she*
> *poured it on Jesus' feet and wiped his feet with her hair. And the*
> *house was filled with the fragrance of the perfume.*
> *⁴But one of his disciples, Judas Iscariot, who was later to*
> *betray him, objected, ⁵"Why wasn't this perfume sold and the*
> *money given to the poor? It was worth a year's wages." ⁶He did*
> *not say this because he cared about the poor but because he was*
> *a thief; as keeper of the money bag, he used to help himself to*
> *what was put into it.*
> *⁷"Leave her alone," Jesus replied. "It was intended that*
> *she should save this perfume for the day of my burial. ⁸You*
> *will always have the poor among you, but you will not always*
> *have me."*
>
> —John 12:1–8

4. What do you learn about Mary's personality from this scene?

5. There is no record that Mary traveled anywhere to preach the gospel. What value does a personality like hers have in the Christian community?

6. What does it say about God that he created people like Paul as well as people like Mary?

DEVELOPING YOUR SHAPE TO SERVE OTHERS 30–40 min.

God loves diverse personalities. All have something to offer in his kingdom. It's helpful to understand your own personality so you can find modes of service that fit you. It's also helpful to understand other people's personalities so you can appreciate them and benefit from their differences. Personality differences can be a source of tension and conflict, or they can be a source of mutual growth.

7. Although there are many fine personality assessments available, you can learn a lot about your design for service if you look at just four basic aspects. Mark where you fall on each of the four scales below.

How are you energized? What recharges your inner batteries?

Extrovert

I get energy from

- being with people.
- working with a team.
- focusing on what is happening *around* me.

Introvert

I get energy from

- having time alone.
- working alone or one-on-one.
- focusing on what is happening *inside* me.

Extroverted   Introverted

3   *2*   *1*   *1*   *2*   *3*

high   low   low   high

What kinds of tasks do you prefer?

Routine

I like tasks that

- are predictable.
- are similar every day.
- require more action than decision.

Variety

I like tasks that

- are unpredictable.
- are different every day.
- require many decisions.

Routine   Variety

3   *2*   *1*   *1*   *2*   *3*

high   low   low   high

How expressive are you?

Self-Controlled

I like to

- reflect before I speak.
- be in control of my moods.
- restrain my reactions.

Self-Expressive

I like to

- express openly what I think
- express openly what I feel
- feel deeply and think strongly

Self-Controlled					Self-Expressive
3	2	1	1	2	3
high		low	low		high

How do you usually relate to others?

Cooperative

I like to

- work together.
- aim for a shared goal.
- not have winners and losers.
- enjoy the process as much as the goal.

Competitive

I like to

- compete against an opponent.
- aim for a goal.
- celebrate victory.
- win.

Cooperative					Competitive
3	2	1	1	2	3
high		low	low		high

8. Record your responses on your SHAPE Worksheet on page 79.

9. (Optional) Take turns sharing your results with the group. How do others see you?

10. Healthy small groups allow people to contribute in different ways according to how God has designed them. Think about your gifts, abilities, and personality. How can you best contribute to your group? Here are some possibilities for each of the church's five purposes:

☐ **CONNECTING**: Plan a social event for the group, *and/or* call unconnected or absent members each week to see how they're doing.

☐ **GROWING**: Encourage personal devotions through group discussions and spiritual (accountability) partners, *and/or* facilitate a three- or four-person discussion during your Bible study next week.

☐ **DEVELOPING**: Ensure that every member finds a group role or responsibility, *and/or* coordinate a group service project in your church or community.

☐ **SHARING**: Collect names of unchurched friends for whom the group could pray and share updates, *and/or* help launch a six-week starter group with other friends or unconnected people.

☐ **SURRENDERING**: Coordinate the group's prayer and praise list (a list of prayer requests and answers to prayer), *and/or* lead the group in a brief worship time, using a CD, video, or instrument.

Note: Most groups find it easy to get people for CONNECTING. It's harder to get people to help with DEVELOPING and SHARING. Would you be willing to help in one of these areas for just sixty days? There's bound to be a way you can help that fits with your gifts, abilities, and personality. You don't have to have the gift of evangelism to help with SHARING!

SURRENDERING YOUR LIFE FOR GOD'S PLEASURE   15–20 min.

11. How can the group pray for you this week? Share prayer requests, but be sure to save time to actually pray! If you prefer to pray silently, you can simply say "amen" to let the group know you're finished.

As you leave, remember

• your goal for the next thirty days.
• to keep on with your daily devotions.
• to hide God's Word in your heart through your weekly Scripture memory verse.

STUDY NOTES

Preach him among the Gentiles. Paul was a religious zealot before he became a follower of Jesus. He lived his whole life with zeal. God used that personality trait of zeal for God's glory by sending Paul to the Gentiles (non-Jews) in uncharted territory throughout what is now Turkey and Greece. This was a tough assignment that needed someone who wouldn't give up easily.

Mary. Mary was the one who sat at Jesus' feet in the account recorded in Luke 10:38–42. When Jesus raised her brother from the dead (John 11), she had even greater reason to love Jesus. She seems to have had a quiet sense that he was the King of Israel *and* that he was facing imminent death.

An expensive perfume. This imported perfume was often used as an investment that could be sold or traded on the open market. It was worth three hundred denarii—about a year's wages. Contrast Mary's sacrifice with Judas's scolding remark. There are times when lavish expression of love for Jesus is worth what it might cost us.

Wiped his feet with her hair. Mary had to get down on her hands and knees in order to get so close to Jesus' feet. For a woman to unbind her hair in public was shocking in that culture, and doing so placed Mary's reputation at risk. Mary's action was extravagant and heedless of humiliation. Our service, too, can require us to get very close and take big risks.

Anoint. The custom of anointing was originally simply a remedy for skin dryness. It later became a symbol of honor, respect, and God's empowering presence when prophets or kings were anointed for their office (1 Samuel 16:12, for example). Bodies were also anointed for burial. Mary was anointing the one she believed to be the rightful King of Israel.

☐ ***For Further Study*** *on this topic, read Philippians 2:1–4; 3:4–14; Luke 7:47; John 13:1–20.*

☐ ***Weekly Memory Verse:*** 2 Timothy 1:6

☐ ***The Purpose-Driven Life Reading Plan:*** Day 33

NOTES

If you're using the DVD along
with this curriculum, please use
this space to take notes on the
teaching for this session.

46

SERVING FROM EXPERIENCE

One summer I took my kids to the pool for a swim. As I settled into my chair, I noticed urgency around me, then panic. A little boy was missing, and everyone was frantically looking for him. They would come to discover that the four-year-old had drowned in the deep end of the pool without anyone noticing. I was sick inside, grieving for the child and his parents.

A few days later Brett and I decided that we *had* to make contact with the parents and try to comfort them in their grief. Brett and I had never experienced a child drowning, but the first precious little girl born to us had died at a very early age, and the sadness was more than we could bear. Our experience gave me such a heart for the parents of this young boy. We felt we wanted them to know that someone cared—that they could go on in life because they were not alone.

From that time on we've stayed connected with them and continue to enjoy their friendship. Nothing ever diminishes our pain and loss, yet our circumstances gave us a heart to love and to comfort this couple.

—Dee

CONNECTING WITH GOD'S FAMILY   10 min.

1. Share with the group a high point in your spiritual experience—perhaps a time when you felt especially close to God, or the specific time when you committed yourself to following Jesus, or a time when you became interested in finding out if God was real.

GROWING TO BE LIKE CHRIST   20 min.

It's often easy to see how the high points of our lives have equipped us to serve God. But it can be harder at times to see how our experiences of failure, sin, betrayal, or violation can become fruitful when we surrender them to God. Take, for example, the following passages, which trace a turning point in the life of the disciple named Peter.

Peter was a passionate follower of Jesus, confident that he would do anything for his Lord. At their last meal before Jesus' arrest, Jesus tried to prepare his followers for the horror that was about to take place. Peter didn't understand what Jesus was talking about, but he was sure he'd be able to handle anything:

> Simon Peter asked him, "Lord, where are you going?"
>
> Jesus replied, "Where I am going, you cannot follow now, but you will follow later."
>
> [37]Peter asked, "Lord, why can't I follow you now? I will lay down my life for you."
>
> [38]Then Jesus answered, "Will you really lay down your life for me? I tell you the truth, before the rooster crows, you will disown me three times!"
>
> —John 13:36–38

Jesus was arrested a few hours later, and Peter fled, along with the other disciples. The soldiers took Jesus to a house for questioning, and Peter slipped into the courtyard with another disciple to try to find out what was going on. The various interrogations went on all throughout the night and until dawn.

> Then the detachment of soldiers with its commander and the Jewish officials arrested Jesus. They bound him [13]and brought him first to Annas, who was the father-in-law of Caiaphas, the high priest that year. [14]Caiaphas was the one who had advised the Jews that it would be good if one man died for the people.
>
> [15]Simon Peter and another disciple were following Jesus. Because this disciple was known to the high priest, he went with Jesus into the high priest's courtyard, [16]but Peter had to wait outside at the door. The other disciple, who was known to the high priest, came back, spoke to the girl on duty there and brought Peter in.

¹⁷"You are not one of his disciples, are you?" the girl at the door asked Peter.

He replied, "I am not."

¹⁸It was cold, and the servants and officials stood around a fire they had made to keep warm. Peter also was standing with them, warming himself.

¹⁹Meanwhile, the high priest questioned Jesus about his disciples and his teaching. . . .

²⁵As Simon Peter stood warming himself, he was asked, "You are not one of his disciples, are you?"

He denied it, saying, "I am not."

²⁶One of the high priest's servants, a relative of the man whose ear Peter had cut off, challenged him, "Didn't I see you with him in the olive grove?" ²⁷Again Peter denied it, and at that moment a rooster began to crow.

—John 18:12–19, 25–27

2. Before Jesus' arrest, how did Peter see himself (John 13:36–38)?

3. What happened in the courtyard that challenged Peter's self-image?

4. If you had been in Peter's shoes, what would have gone through your mind when people began asking if you were one of Jesus' disciples?

5. How would you have felt when the rooster crowed?

Jesus was crucified that very afternoon. Three days later he rose from the dead! Peter's despair turned to joy, but the memory of his failure continued to haunt him.

For forty days Jesus showed up periodically to visit with and to train his disciples. The following passage describes something that happened during one of those visits. Peter and some other disciples were fishing, and Jesus appeared on the shore. The disciples headed for shore, and Jesus cooked them fish for breakfast:

> When they had finished eating, Jesus said to Simon Peter, "Simon son of John, do you truly love me more than these?"
>
> "Yes, Lord," he said, "you know that I love you."
>
> Jesus said, "Feed my lambs."
>
> [16]Again Jesus said, "Simon son of John, do you truly love me?"
>
> He answered, "Yes, Lord, you know that I love you."
>
> Jesus said, "Take care of my sheep."
>
> [17]The third time he said to him, "Simon son of John, do you love me?"
>
> Peter was hurt because Jesus asked him the third time, "Do you love me?" He said, "Lord, you know all things; you know that I love you."
>
> Jesus said, "Feed my sheep. [18]I tell you the truth, when you were younger you dressed yourself and went where you wanted; but when you are old you will stretch out your hands, and someone else will dress you and lead you where you do not want to go." [19]Jesus said this to indicate the kind of death by which Peter would glorify God. Then he said to him, "Follow me!"
>
> —John 21:15–19

6. Three times Peter denied that he knew Jesus. Three times Jesus asked Peter, "Do you love me?" Why do you think Jesus did that?

7. What do you think Peter was feeling throughout this scene?

8. Look back at what Peter said in John 13:36–38. Compare his words in John 21:15–19. How do you think this whole experience affected Peter's character?

9. How might this experience have helped equip Peter to "feed [Jesus'] sheep"?

DEVELOPING YOUR SHAPE TO SERVE OTHERS   10–15 min.

Peter's story shows that brokenness can be a blessing. A cocky young man can become a wise and gentle shepherd of people through experiences of grief and a willingness to learn from failure and to gain self-understanding. We all need to embrace our past experiences, both positive and painful, and allow God to use them to shape us so as to fulfill his purpose.

10. Take about ten minutes to reflect on your most significant life experiences. Write some notes on one experience in each of the four categories below. Choose experiences you think have helped shape the person God has created you to be.

Spiritual Experience

Painful Experience (a trial or problem you've experienced that you could use to encourage another person)

Educational or Work Experience (a school, seminar, job, or training experience)

Ministry Experience (an area in which you've served in the past, if any)

On the SHAPE Worksheet on pages 78–79, locate the Experiences section and write brief notes to remind you of some of the key experiences that have shaped you.

SURRENDERING YOUR LIFE FOR GOD'S PLEASURE   45 min.

11. Sit next to your spiritual partner(s). Together do one or more of the following:

    • Share what you learned from your devotional time this week.
    • Recite your memory verse.
    • Tell how you're doing with the goal you set for yourself.

12. Share with your group one of the experiences you noted in question 10. Choose one that has had a great impact on who you are today. You can choose one that you think God can use for his purposes, or you can choose one that you can't imagine God using for good.

    As each person shares, group members can offer affirmation as to how God might use that experience to bring good to others. Take a moment to pray for the person. Pray that God will enable each of you to see *every part* of your life, positive or painful, as part of his master design and as part of the fulfillment of your unique role as his servant.

STUDY NOTES

Simon Peter and another disciple were following Jesus. A disciple (*mathētes* in Greek) is a learner and a follower of a teacher. Like a child with a parent, a disciple learns from and follows the teacher's lead. Discipleship requires that one has determined ahead of time the cost of studying under and following a rabbinical teacher like Jesus. It does not mean that one is perfect—only *committed*. Peter made that decision to follow Jesus, even though Peter made a number of mistakes along the way (Matthew 16:22–28; 17:4–5).

I am not. Peter repeated these three words three times. They embody a great blunder. But Peter learned from his mistakes—note his recovery as demonstrated in John 21:15–22; Acts 2:14; 3:6, 16; 4:8–20. Peter's failures built strength and character into his life, which he came to rely on later. Failure didn't build character automatically; a key element was the way in which Peter dealt with failure, namely, through a repentant heart and a willingness to learn from mistakes.

☐ *For Further Study* on this topic, read Matthew 16:22–28; 17:4–5; John 21:15–22; Acts 2:14; 3:6, 16; 4:8–20.

☐ *Weekly Memory Verse:* Genesis 50:20

☐ *The Purpose-Driven Life Reading Plan:* Day 34

NOTES

If you're using the DVD along with this curriculum, please use this space to take notes on the teaching for this session.

55

6 SERVING WITH YOUR WHOLE HEART

I love reading nonfiction adventures. They inspire me to live out my dream rather than to just settle for mediocrity. One such story is that of Ernest Shackleton, an explorer who coordinated the British Imperial Trans-Antarctic Expedition to cross the Antarctic continent for the first time.

In December 1914, Shackleton set sail with his twenty-seven–man crew. Many of them had responded to the following recruitment notice: "Men wanted for hazardous journey. Small wages. Bitter cold. Long months of complete darkness. Constant danger. Safe return doubtful. Honour and recognition in case of success." The response to this ad had been overwhelming. Shackleton said, "It seemed as though every man in Great Britain was determined to accompany me."

Battling the winter ice, disastrous occurrences, starvation, and isolation, Shackleton and his men pressed on to accomplish the impossible—and lived to tell about it. I wonder if I would have been willing to go along for the adventure. As I consider my own gifts, I realize that God has given me talents to invest, and yet I often lose my zeal to go along for the adventure. Doing the work of God in a fallen world is as great and harrowing an adventure as crossing Antarctica, and I desire so much to respond like the men of Great Britain. I want to be ready to risk everything and to be willing to serve with my whole heart in order to do the work God wants done.

—Todd

CONNECTING WITH GOD'S FAMILY   10 min.

You can serve with your gifts, your abilities, and your temperament, but there's one more piece of your SHAPE that can keep you going for the long haul, namely, *your heart*. How has God shaped your heart—what you love to do, or what you're passionate about?

1. If you had all the resources and knew you couldn't fail, what is one thing you would try to do for God with your life?

God places certain interests, desires, and passions in our hearts. Living out his plan is exhilarating, yet some days it feels like hard work and drudgery. Even on the days that seem mundane, we have more energy to persist if we know we're serving in an area we care about and if we're living out part of God's plan.

Your heart is the core of you—the center of your desires, motives, feelings, attitudes, and inclinations. When you feel passionate about something God also feels passionate about, then you have a strong clue that it's something you should pursue. What makes you weep, or pound the table? What gives you joy? What do you ache to see God accomplish? If the answer is "nothing," you're a very different person from the apostle Paul. Here he describes the passion that burns in his heart:

> I want you to know how glad I am that it's me sitting here in this jail and not you. There's a lot of suffering to be entered into in this world—the kind of suffering Christ takes on. I welcome the chance to take my share in the church's part of that suffering. 25When I became a servant in this church, I experienced this suffering as a sheer gift, God's way of helping me serve you, laying out the whole truth.
>
> 26This mystery has been kept in the dark for a long time, but now it's out in the open. 27God wanted everyone, not just Jews, to know this rich and glorious secret inside and out, regardless of their background, regardless of their religious standing. The mystery in a nutshell is just this: Christ is in you, therefore you can look forward to sharing in God's glory. It's that simple. That is the substance of our Message. 28We preach Christ, warning people not to add to the Message. We teach in a spirit of profound common sense so that we can bring each person to maturity. To be mature is to be basic. Christ! No more, no less. 29That's what I'm working so hard at day after day, year after year, doing my best with the energy God so generously gives me.
>
> 2:1I want you to realize that I continue to work as hard as I know how for you, and also for the Christians over at Laodicea.
>
> —Colossians 1:24–2:1 THE MESSAGE

2. What desire burns in Paul's heart?

3. What is he willing to go through in order to see his desire achieved?

4. Think about this: "Christ is in you, therefore you can look forward to sharing in God's glory" (verse 27). What do you envision "God's glory" will be like when you share in it?

5. What does it mean to "bring each person to maturity" (verse 28)?

6. What goes on inside you when you think about how passionate Paul is about his goal? (For instance, are you that passionate about anything, or does this kind of passion seem like something you could never have?)

DEVELOPING YOUR SHAPE TO SERVE OTHERS

Not everyone is as emotional as Paul. But *everyone* has a heart that is passionate about something. However, many people have learned to disconnect from their heart's desires in order to avoid suffering the anguish of disappointment and failure. Paul *really* wanted to see people become perfectly glorious in Jesus Christ, so he was *really* disappointed when people backed away from the fullness of what Jesus wanted for them. He risked great pain and crushing failure, even the agony of being confined in jail. Many of us would rather not hurt in those ways, so we settle for doing what's safe rather than what draws our hearts. If we do it long enough, we may succeed in numbing our passions or settling for lesser passions like food or television. Then we wonder why life bores us, or why we can't seem to resist our favorite temptations.

7. *(Optional)* If you don't know how your heart desires to serve God, there are a number of things you can do to find out. One clue is remembering what you enjoyed doing in the past.

    What is one thing you *accomplished* as a child that you *enjoyed* doing?

8. Think about your answer to question 1, and factor in the rest of what you know about yourself. Which of the following words best describes something you are passionate about?
    I am passionate to

    ☐ design/develop.   ☐ pioneer.
    ☐ organize.   ☐ operate/maintain.
    ☐ serve/help.   ☐ acquire/possess.
    ☐ excel.   ☐ perform.
    ☐ improve.   ☐ repair.
    ☐ lead/be in charge.   ☐ persevere.
    ☐ follow the rules.   ☐ prevail.
    ☐ influence.

    You can check the appropriate box in the Heart section on your SHAPE Worksheet on page 78.

9. Share with the group what you love to do or what you're passionate about. It doesn't have to be as dramatic as bringing the whole world to know Jesus Christ. It doesn't have to be the perfect description. It can even sound silly. Just share what comes to mind.

10. Now rubber meets road. Look at your SHAPE worksheet on pages 78–79. What area of ministry will you test-drive during the next three months? Knowing what you now know about your SHAPE, what will you try first? Here are some ideas for ministry areas; feel free to invite other ideas from your group members:

   ☐ your church's worship department: performing, doing office work . . .
   ☐ your church's children and youth department: teaching, mentoring, doing office work, making phone calls, doing curriculum design, participating in art activities, loving the kids, helping to plan and carry out special events . . .
   ☐ small groups: being a leader, doing some coordinating, being an organizer, helping to plan and carry out socials, being an encourager, making phone calls . . .
   ☐ helping the poor: collecting food and goods, distributing needed items, organizing volunteers, doing training, helping in publicity . . .
   ☐ your community: building relationships with non-Christians, tutoring kids, helping an elderly neighbor, counseling pregnant teens . . .
   ☐ your ideas:

SURRENDERING YOUR LIFE FOR GOD'S PLEASURE   10–30 min.

11. What's next for your group? Turn to the Purpose-Driven Group Agreement on page 67. Do you want to agree to continue meeting together? If so, do you want to change anything in this agreement (times, dates, shared values, and so on)? Are there any things you'd like the group to do better as it moves forward? Take notes on this discussion.

12. Place a chair in the center of the room and invite each person in turn to sit in the chair. The other group members will place their hands on this person and pray for him or her. Ask God to empower him or her for the area of ministry being undertaken. Ask God to use this opportunity to reveal gifts, abilities, personality, and heart. Pray for a servant's heart and for fruitful results. The person can also share any personal prayer requests. When all members have been prayed for (including the leader!), close with a time of thanksgiving for what you've gained from this study.

STUDY NOTES

Suffering. Affliction, either emotional or physical. Everyone on earth suffers. It's an inescapable part of life, and Christians are not exempt. In fact, serving God often involves putting ourselves in harm's way for the sake of something profoundly important. We actually do our best service when we are stretched beyond our own resources and forced to rely on God for the strength to endure.

God's way of helping me serve you. "Stewardship" (NASB) or *oikonomia* (Greek). A steward manages an estate for another. We are stewards or managers of God's property—first the community of God's people, and ultimately the whole earth. We are all stewards, all called to help manage God's property in one way or another.

Mystery. In the Bible a mystery is not a puzzle to solve or a secret to be kept. Rather, it's something astonishing that has long been secret but now should be announced from the rooftops. *Christ* is the great mystery, the surprise that shocked even angels when he became human and died for humans.

Preach . . . warning . . . teach. These words express Paul's unique SHAPE. Preaching, or proclamation, is the formal declaration of the gospel in a public setting. Warning, or admonishing, means to caution or reprove gently. Teaching is biblical instruction.

Bring each person to maturity. "Present everyone perfect in Christ" (NIV). The Greek word *teleios* means "perfect," or "mature." Something is *teleios* if it reaches the form or goal it was made for. A tree is *teleios* when it is fully grown and bearing fruit. A person is *teleios* when he or she is fully the person God intended, manifesting the character and actions he or she was born for.

That's what I'm working so hard at day after day, year after year, doing my best. Paul was willing to "labor" (NASB), to weary himself with extended effort. We labor in what we believe in. Laboring is giving our heart, soul, and strength to an effort. Paul was also willing to "struggle" (NASB). Struggling, or "doing my best," renders the Greek word *agōnizomenos*, from which we get our English word *agonize*. It's an athletic term to describe intense exertion.

☐ ***For Further Study*** *on this topic, read Matthew 25:14–30.*

☐ ***Weekly Memory Verse:*** Matthew 19:26

☐ ***The Purpose-Driven Life Reading Plan:*** Day 35

If you're using the DVD along
with this curriculum, please use
this space to take notes on the
teaching for this session.

FREQUENTLY ASKED QUESTIONS

Who may attend the group?

Anybody you feel would benefit from it. As you begin, we encourage each attender to invite at least one other friend to join. A good time to join is in the first or second week of a new study. Share the names of your friends with the group members so that they can be praying for you.

How long will this group meet?

It's totally up to the group—once you come to the end of this six-week study. Most groups meet weekly for at least the first six weeks, but every other week can work as well. At the end of this study, each group member may decide if he or she wants to continue on for another six-week study. We encourage you to consider using the next study in this series. The series is designed to take you on a developmental journey to healthy, purpose-driven lives in thirty-six sessions. However, each guide stands on its own and may be taken in any order. You may take a break between studies if you wish.

Who is the leader?

This booklet will walk you through every step for an effective group. In addition, your group may have selected one or more discussion leaders. We strongly recommend that you rotate the job of facilitating your discussions so that everyone's gifts can emerge and develop. You can share other responsibilities as well, such as bringing refreshments or keeping up with those who miss a meeting. There's no reason why one or two people need to do everything; in fact, sharing ownership of the group will help *everyone* grow. Finally, the Bible says that when two or more are gathered in Jesus' name (which you are), he is there in your midst. Ultimately, God is your leader each step of the way.

Where do we find new members for our group?

This can be troubling, especially for new groups that have only a few people or for existing groups that lose a few people along the way. We encourage you to pray with your group and then brainstorm a list of people from work, church, your neighborhood, your children's school, family, the gym, and so forth. Then have each group member invite several of the people on their list. Another good strategy is to ask church leaders to make an announcement or to allow for a bulletin insert.

No matter how you find members, it's vital that you stay on the lookout for new people to join your group. All groups tend to go through some amount of healthy attrition—the result of moves, releasing new leaders, ministry opportunities, and so forth—and if the group gets too small, it could be at risk of shutting down. If you and your group stay open, you'll be amazed at the people God sends your way. The next person just might become a friend for life. You never know!

How do we handle the child care needs in our group?

Very carefully. Seriously, this can be a sensitive issue. We suggest that you empower the group to openly brainstorm solutions. You may try something that works for some and not for others, so you must just keep playing with the dials. One common solution is to meet in the living room or dining room with the adults and to share the cost of a baby-sitter (or two) who can be with the kids in a different part of the house. Another popular option is to use one home for the kids and a second home (close by or a phone call away) for the adults. Finally, you could rotate the responsibility of providing a lesson of some sort for the kids. This last idea can be an incredible blessing to you and the kids. We've done it, and it's worked great! Again, the best approach is to encourage the group to dialogue openly about both the problem and the solution.

PURPOSE-DRIVEN GROUP AGREEMENT

It's a good idea for every group to put words to their shared values, expectations, and commitments. A written agreement will help you avoid unspoken agendas and disappointed expectations. You'll discuss your agreement in session 1, and then you'll revisit it in session 6 to decide whether you want to modify anything as you move forward as a group. (Alternatively, you may agree to end your group in session 6.) Feel free to modify anything that doesn't work for your group.

If the idea of having a written agreement is unfamiliar to your group, we encourage you to give it a try. A clear agreement is invaluable for resolving conflict constructively and for setting your group on a path to health.

We agree to the following values:

Clear Purpose   To grow healthy spiritual lives by building a healthy small group community. In addition, we _____

_____

_____

_____

_____

Group Attendance   To give priority to the group meeting (call if I will be late or absent)

Safe Environment   To help create a safe place where people can be heard and feel loved (please, no quick answers, snap judgments, or simple fixes)

Confidentiality   To keep anything that is shared strictly confidential and within the group

Spiritual Health   To give group members permission to help me live a healthy spiritual life that is pleasing to God (see the health assessment and health plan)

Inviting People	To keep an open chair in our group and share Jesus' dream of finding a shepherd for every sheep by inviting newcomers
Shared Ownership	To remember that every member is a minister and to encourage each attender to share a small group role or serve on one of the purpose teams (page 70)
Rotating Leaders	To encourage someone new to facilitate the group each week and to rotate homes and refreshments as well (see Small Group Calendar)
Spiritual Partners	To pair up with one other group member whom I can support more diligently and help to grow spiritually (my spiritual partner is _____)

We agree to the following expectations:

- Refreshments/Mealtimes _____

- Child care _____

- When we will meet (day of week) _____

- Where we will meet (place) _____

- We will begin at (time)_____ and end at _____

- We will do our best to have some or all of us attend a worship service together. Our primary worship service time will be _____

- Review date of this agreement: _____

We agree to the following commitment:

Father, to the best of my ability, in light of what I know to be true, I commit the next season of my life to CONNECTING with your family, GROWING to be more like Christ, DEVELOPING my shape for ministry, SHARING my life mission every day, and SURRENDERING my life for your pleasure.

_____	_____	_____
Name	Date	Spiritual Partner (witness)

SMALL GROUP CALENDAR

Healthy purpose-driven groups share responsibilities and group ownership. This usually doesn't happen overnight but progressively over time. Sharing responsibilities and ownership ensures that no one person carries the group alone. The calendar below can help you in this area. You can also add a social event, mission project, birthdays, or days off to your calendar. This should be completed after your first or second meeting. Planning ahead will facilitate better attendance and greater involvement from others.

Date	Lesson	Location	Dessert/Meal	Facilitator
Monday, January 15	1	Steve and Laura's	Joe	Bill

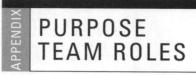

PURPOSE TEAM ROLES

The Bible makes clear that every member, not just the small group leader, is a minister in the body of Christ. In a purpose-driven small group (just like in a purpose-driven church), every member plays a role on the team. Review the team roles and responsibilities below and have each member volunteer for a role, or have the group suggest a role for each member. It's best to have one or two people on each team, so you have each purpose covered. Serving in even a small capacity will not only help your leader grow but will also make the group more fun for everyone. Don't hold back. Join a team!

The opportunities below are broken down by the five purposes and then by a *crawl* (beginning group role), *walk* (intermediate group role), or *run* (advanced group role). Try to cover the crawl and walk phases if you can.

Purpose Team Roles	Purpose Team Members
Fellowship Team (**CONNECTING** with God's Family)	
Crawl: Host social events or group activities	_____
Walk: Serve as a small group inviter	_____
Run: Lead the CONNECTING time each week	_____
Discipleship Team (**GROWING** to Be Like Christ)	
Crawl: Ensure that each member has a simple plan and a partner for personal devotions	_____
Walk: Disciple a few younger group members	_____
Run: Facilitate the Purpose-Driven Life Health Assessment and Purpose-Driven Life Health Plan processes	_____

Ministry Team (**DEVELOPING** Your Shape for Ministry)

Crawl: Ensure that each member finds a group role _____
or a purpose team responsibility

Walk: Plan a ministry project for the group in the _____
church or community

Run: Help each member discover and develop _____
a SHAPE-based ministry in the church

Evangelism (Missions) Team (**SHARING** Your Life Mission Every Day)

Crawl: Coordinate the group prayer and praise list _____
of non-Christian friends and family members

Walk: Pray for group mission opportunities and _____
plan a group cross-cultural adventure

Run: Plan as a group to attend a holiday service, _____
host a neighborhood party, or create a seeker
event for your non-Christian friends

Worship Team (**SURRENDERING** Your Life for God's Pleasure)

Crawl: Maintain the weekly group prayer and praise _____
list or journal

Walk: Lead a brief worship time in your group _____
(CD/video/a cappella)

Run: Plan a Communion time, prayer walk, foot _____
washing, or an outdoor worship experience

PURPOSE-DRIVEN LIFE HEALTH ASSESSMENT

	Just Beginning	Getting Going	Well Developed

CONNECTING WITH GOD'S FAMILY

I am deepening my understanding of and friendship with God in community with others — 1 2 3 4 5

I am growing in my ability both to share and to show my love to others — 1 2 3 4 5

I am willing to share my real needs for prayer and support from others — 1 2 3 4 5

I am resolving conflict constructively and am willing to forgive others — 1 2 3 4 5

CONNECTING Total _____

GROWING TO BE LIKE CHRIST

I have a growing relationship with God through regular time in the Bible and in prayer (spiritual habits) — 1 2 3 4 5

I am experiencing more of the characteristics of Jesus Christ (love, joy, peace, patience, kindness, self-control, etc.) in my life — 1 2 3 4 5

I am avoiding addictive behaviors (food, television, busyness, and the like) to meet my needs — 1 2 3 4 5

I am spending time with a Christian friend (spiritual partner) who celebrates and challenges my spiritual growth — 1 2 3 4 5

GROWING Total _____

DEVELOPING YOUR SHAPE TO SERVE OTHERS

I have discovered and am further developing my unique God-given shape for ministry — 1 2 3 4 5

I am regularly praying for God to show me opportunities to serve him and others — 1 2 3 4 5

I am serving in a regular (once a month or more) ministry in the church or community — 1 2 3 4 5

I am a team player in my small group by sharing some group role or responsibility — 1 2 3 4 5

DEVELOPING Total_____

SHARING YOUR LIFE MISSION EVERY DAY

I am cultivating relationships with non-Christians and praying
for God to give me natural opportunities to share his love   1 2 3 4 5

I am investing my time in another person or group who needs
to know Christ personally   1 2 3 4 5

I am regularly inviting unchurched or unconnected friends to
my church or small group   1 2 3 4 5

I am praying and learning about where God can use me and
our group cross-culturally for missions   1 2 3 4 5

SHARING Total _____

SURRENDERING YOUR LIFE FOR GOD'S PLEASURE

I am experiencing more of the presence and power of God in
my everyday life   1 2 3 4 5

I am faithfully attending my small group and weekend services
to worship God   1 2 3 4 5

I am seeking to please God by surrendering every area of my life
(health, decisions, finances, relationships, future, etc.) to him   1 2 3 4 5

I am accepting the things I cannot change and becoming
increasingly grateful for the life I've been given   1 2 3 4 5

SURRENDERING Total_____

Total your scores for each purpose, and place them on the chart below. Reassess
your progress at the end of thirty days. Be sure to select your spiritual partner and
the one area in which you'd like to make progress over the next thirty days.

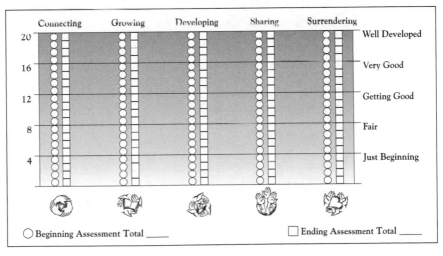

PURPOSE-DRIVEN LIFE HEALTH PLAN

My Name _____ Date _____

My Spiritual Partner _____ Date _____

Possibilities

Plan
(make one goal for each area)

 CONNECTING WITH GOD'S FAMILY
Hebrews 10:24–25; Ephesians 2:19
How can I deepen my relationships with others?

- Attend my group more faithfully

- Schedule lunch with a group member

- Begin praying for a spiritual mentor

WHO is/are my shepherd(s)?

NAME: _____

GROWING TO BE LIKE CHRIST
Colossians 1:28; Ephesians 4:15
How can I grow to be like Christ?

- Commit to personal time with God three days a week

- Ask a friend for devotional accountability

- Begin journaling my prayers

WHAT is my Spiritual Health Plan?

RENEWAL DATE: _____

DEVELOPING YOUR SHAPE TO SERVE OTHERS
Ephesians 4:11–13; 1 Corinthians 12:7; 1 Peter 3:10
How can I develop my shape for ministry?

- Begin praying for a personal ministry

- Attend a gift discovery class

- Serve together at a church event or in the community

WHERE am I serving others?

MINISTRY: _____

SHARING YOUR LIFE MISSION EVERY DAY
Matthew 28:18–20; Acts 20:24
How can I share my faith every day?

- Start meeting for lunch with a seeker friend

- Invite a non-Christian relative to church

- Pray for and support an overseas missionary

WHEN am I sharing my life mission?

TIME: _____

SURRENDERING YOUR LIFE FOR GOD'S PLEASURE
How can I surrender my life for God's pleasure?

- Submit one area to God

- Be honest about my struggle and hurt

- Buy a music CD for worship in my car and in the group

HOW am I surrendering my life today?

AREA: _____

	Progress (renew and revise)	Progress (renew and revise)	Progress (renew and revise)
	30 days/Date _____ ☐ ☐ ☐ ☐ Weekly check-in with my spiritual partner or group	60-90 days/Date _____ ☐ ☐ ☐ ☐ Weekly check-in with my spiritual partner or group	120+ days/Date _____ ☐ ☐ ☐ ☐ Weekly check-in with my spiritual partner or group
CONNECTING			
GROWING			
DEVELOPING			
SHARING			
SURRENDERING			

SPIRITUAL PARTNERS'
CHECK-IN PAGE

My Name _____   Spiritual Partner's Name _____

	Our Plans	Our Progress
Week 1		
Week 2		
Week 3		
Week 4		
Week 5		
Week 6		

Briefly check in each week and write down your personal plans and progress for the next week (or even for the next few weeks). This could be done (before or after the meeting) on the phone, through an E-mail message, or even in person from time to time.

SHAPE
WORKSHEET

God has designed you with a unique SHAPE. Your SHAPE enables you to serve God in ways no other person can. It makes you irreplaceable. If you know your SHAPE, you'll have many clues about the service to which God is calling you. Discerning God's will for your life becomes much easier.

This worksheet will help you discover and develop your SHAPE. By the end of session 6, you will have all five areas filled out. You will also have feedback from your group members that affirms what they see in you for each area. Use this worksheet as a guideline for choosing ministry both inside and outside your group.

Spiritual Gifts

- [ ] Preaching
- [ ] Evangelism
- [ ] Discernment
- [ ] Apostle
- [ ] Teaching
- [ ] Encouragement
- [ ] Wisdom
- [ ] Missions
- [ ] Service
- [ ] Mercy
- [ ] Hospitality
- [ ] Pastoring
- [ ] Giving
- [ ] Intercession
- [ ] Music
- [ ] Arts and Crafts
- [ ] Healing
- [ ] Miracles
- [ ] Leadership
- [ ] Administration
- [ ] Faith

Heart—I Love to

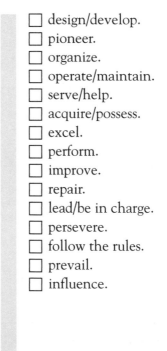

- [ ] design/develop.
- [ ] pioneer.
- [ ] organize.
- [ ] operate/maintain.
- [ ] serve/help.
- [ ] acquire/possess.
- [ ] excel.
- [ ] perform.
- [ ] improve.
- [ ] repair.
- [ ] lead/be in charge.
- [ ] persevere.
- [ ] follow the rules.
- [ ] prevail.
- [ ] influence.

Abilities

- ☐ Entertaining
- ☐ Recruiting
- ☐ Interviewing
- ☐ Researching
- ☐ Artistic/Graphics
- ☐ Evaluating
- ☐ Planning
- ☐ Managing
- ☐ Counseling
- ☐ Teaching
- ☐ Writing/Editing
- ☐ Promoting
- ☐ Repairing
- ☐ Feeding
- ☐ Recall
- ☐ Mechanical Operating
- ☐ Resourceful
- ☐ Counting/Classifying
- ☐ Public Relations
- ☐ Welcoming
- ☐ Composing
- ☐ Landscaping
- ☐ Arts and Crafts
- ☐ Decorating
- ☐ Musical
- ☐
- ☐

Experiences

- ☐ Spiritual:

- ☐ Painful:

- ☐ Education:

- ☐ Work:

- ☐ Ministry:

Personality

	Hi	Lo	Lo	Hi	
Introverted	☐	☐	☐	☐	Extroverted
Variety	☐	☐	☐	☐	Routine
Self-Expressive	☐	☐	☐	☐	Self-Controlled
Competitive	☐	☐	☐	☐	Cooperative

MEMORY VERSES

APPENDIX

One of the most effective ways to instill biblical truth deep into our lives is to memorize key Scriptures. For many, memorization is a new concept—or perhaps one we found difficult in the past. We encourage you to stretch yourself and try to memorize these six verses.

A good way to memorize a verse is to copy it on a sheet of paper five times. Most people learn something by heart when they do this. It's also helpful to post the verse someplace where you will see it several times a day.

WEEK ONE

"I praise you because I am fearfully
     and wonderfully made;
your works are wonderful,
I know that full well."
                    Psalm 139:14

WEEK TWO

"Whoever wants to become great among you must be your servant."
                    Mark 10:43

WEEK THREE

"Each one should use whatever gift he has received to serve others, faithfully administering God's grace in its various forms."
                    1 Peter 4:10

WEEK FOUR

"For this reason I remind you to fan into flame the gift of God, which is in you through the laying on of my hands."
                    2 Timothy 1:6

WEEK FIVE

"You intended to harm me, but God intended it for good to accomplish what is now being done, the saving of many lives."
                    Genesis 50:20

WEEK SIX

"Jesus looked at them and said, 'With man this is impossible, but with God all things are possible.'"
                    Matthew 19:26

DAILY DEVOTIONAL READINGS

We've experienced so much life change as a result of reading the Bible daily. Hundreds of people have gone through DOING LIFE TOGETHER, and they tell us that the number-one contributor to their growth was the deeper walk with God that came as a result of the daily devotions. We strongly encourage you to have everyone set a realistic goal for the six weeks. Pair people into same-gender spiritual (accountability) partners. This will improve your results tenfold. Then we encourage everyone to take a few minutes each day to **READ** the verse for the day, **REFLECT** on what God is saying to you through the verse, and **RESPOND** to God in prayer in a personal journal. Each of these verses was selected to align with the week's study. After you complete the reading, simply put a check mark in the box next to the verse. Enjoy the journey!

WEEK ONE
- [ ] 1 Corinthians 15:58
- [ ] Ephesians 2:4–10
- [ ] Isaiah 45:9–12
- [ ] Genesis 1:27–31
- [ ] Psalm 8:3–9

WEEK TWO
- [ ] Matthew 20:20–28
- [ ] Luke 14:7–11
- [ ] Luke 14:12–14
- [ ] John 13:1–11
- [ ] John 13:12–17

WEEK THREE
- [ ] 1 Peter 4:10–11
- [ ] Ephesians 4:11–13
- [ ] 1 Corinthians 12:4–11
- [ ] Romans 12:4–8
- [ ] Acts 20:24

WEEK FOUR
- [ ] Matthew 5:13–16
- [ ] Job 10:8–12
- [ ] Jeremiah 1:4–8
- [ ] Amos 7:12–15
- [ ] Judges 6:11–16

WEEK FIVE
- [ ] 1 Corinthians 10:31
- [ ] Acts 20:24
- [ ] 2 Timothy 1:6–7
- [ ] Philippians 3:12–14
- [ ] Romans 8:28

WEEK SIX
- [ ] Colossians 3:22–24
- [ ] Ephesians 6:5–8
- [ ] Esther 4:12–16
- [ ] 1 Kings 8:61
- [ ] Deuteronomy 30:11–20

PRAYER AND
PRAISE REPORT

Briefly share your prayer requests with the large group, making notations below. Then gather in small groups of two, three, or four to pray for each need.

	Prayer Request	Praise Report
Week 1		
Week 2		
Week 3		

	Prayer Request	Praise Report
Week 4		
Week 5		
Week 6		

SAMPLE JOURNAL PAGE

Today's Passage: _____

Reflections from my HEART:

    I *Honor* who you are. (Praise God for something.)

    I *Express* who I'm not. (Confess any known sin.)

    I *Affirm* who I am in you. (How does God see you?)

    I *Request* your will for me. (Ask God for something.)

    I *Thank* you for what you've done. (Thank him for something.)

Today's Action Step:

LEADERSHIP
TRAINING

Small Group Leadership 101 (Top Ten Ideas for New Facilitators)

Congratulations! You have responded to the call to help shepherd Jesus' flock. There are few other tasks in the family of God that surpass the contribution you will be making. As you prepare to lead—whether it is one session or the entire series—here are a few thoughts to keep in mind. We encourage you to read these and review them with each new discussion leader before he or she leads.

1. **Remember that you are not alone.** God knows everything about you, and he knew that you would be asked to lead your group. Even though you may not feel ready to lead, this is common for all good leaders. Moses, Solomon, Jeremiah, or Timothy—they *all* were reluctant to lead. God promises, "Never will I leave you; never will I forsake you" (Hebrews 13:5). Whether you are leading for one evening, for several weeks, or for a lifetime, you will be blessed as you serve.

2. **Don't try to do it alone.** Pray right now for God to help you build a healthy leadership team. If you can enlist a coleader to help you lead the group, you will find your experience to be much richer. This is your chance to involve as many people as you can in building a healthy group. All you have to do is call and ask people to help—you'll be surprised at the response.

3. **Just be yourself.** If you won't be you, who will? God wants to use your unique gifts and temperament. Don't try to do things exactly like another leader; do them in a way that fits you! Just admit it when you don't have an answer and apologize when you make a mistake. Your group will love you for it!—and you'll sleep better at night.

4. **Prepare for your meeting ahead of time.** Review the session and the leader's notes, and write down your responses to each question. Pay special attention to exercises that ask group members to do something other than engage in discussion. These exercises will help your group *live* what the Bible teaches, not just talk about it. Be sure you understand how an exercise works, and bring any necessary supplies (such as paper or pens) to your meeting. If the exercise employs one of the items in the appendix (such as the Purpose-Driven Life Health Assessment), be sure to look over that item so

you'll know how it works. Finally, review "Read Me First" on pages 11–14 so you'll remember the purpose of each section in the study.

5. **Pray for your group members by name.** Before you begin your session, go around the room in your mind and pray for each member by name. You may want to review the prayer list at least once a week. Ask God to use your time together to touch the heart of every person uniquely. Expect God to lead you to whomever he wants you to encourage or challenge in a special way. If you listen, God will surely lead!

6. **When you ask a question, be patient.** Someone will eventually respond. Sometimes people need a moment or two of silence to think about the question, and if silence doesn't bother you, it won't bother anyone else. After someone responds, affirm the response with a simple "thanks" or "good job." Then ask, "How about somebody else?" or "Would someone who hasn't shared like to add anything?" Be sensitive to new people or reluctant members who aren't ready to say, pray, or do anything. If you give them a safe setting, they will blossom over time.

7. **Provide transitions between questions.** When guiding the discussion, always read aloud the transitional paragraphs and the questions. Ask the group if anyone would like to read the paragraph or Bible passage. Don't call on anyone, but ask for a volunteer, and then be patient until someone begins. Be sure to thank the person who reads aloud.

8. **Break up into small groups each week, or they won't stay.** If your group has more than seven people, we strongly encourage you to have the group gather in discussion circles of three or four people during the GROWING or SURRENDERING sections of the study. With a greater opportunity to talk in a small circle, people will connect more with the study, apply more quickly what they're learning, and ultimately get more out of it. A small circle also encourages a quiet person to participate and tends to minimize the effects of a more vocal or dominant member. And it can help people feel more loved in your group. When you gather again at the end of the section, you can have one person summarize the highlights from each circle.

Small circles are also helpful during prayer time. People who are unaccustomed to praying aloud will feel more comfortable trying it with just two or three others. Also, prayer requests won't take as much time, so circles will have more time to actually pray. When you gather back with the whole group, you can have one person from each circle briefly update everyone on the prayer requests. People are more willing to pray in small circles if they know that the whole group will hear all the prayer requests.

9. **Rotate facilitators weekly.** At the end of each meeting, ask the group who should lead the following week. Let the group help select your weekly facilitator. You may be perfectly capable of leading each time, but you will help others grow in their faith and gifts if you give them opportunities to lead. You can use the Small Group Calendar on page 69 to fill in the names of all six meeting leaders at once if you prefer.

10. **One final challenge (for new or first-time leaders): Before your first opportunity to lead, look up each of the five passages listed below.** Read each one as a devotional exercise to help prepare yourself with a shepherd's heart. Trust us on this one. If you do this, you will be more than ready for your first meeting.

- ☐ Matthew 9:36
- ☐ 1 Peter 5:2-4
- ☐ Psalm 23
- ☐ Ezekiel 34:11–16
- ☐ 1 Thessalonians 2:7–8, 11–12

Small Group Leadership Lifters (Weekly Leadership Tips)

And David shepherded them with integrity of heart;
with skillful hands he led them.

Psalm 78:73

David provides a model of a leader who has a heart for God, a desire to shepherd God's people, and a willingness to develop the skills of a leader. The following is a series of practical tips for new and existing small group leaders. These principles and practices have proved to cultivate healthy, balanced groups in over a thousand examples.

1. Don't Leave Home without It: A Leader's Prayer

"The prayer of a righteous man [or woman] is powerful and effective" (James 5:16). From the very beginning of this study, why not commit to a simple prayer of renewal in your heart and in the hearts of your members? Take a moment right now and write a simple prayer as you begin:

Father, help me _____

_____

_____

2. Pay It Now or Pay It Later: Group Conflict

Most leaders and groups avoid conflict, but healthy groups are willing to do what it takes to learn and grow through conflict. Much group conflict can be avoided if the leader lets the group openly discuss and decide its direction, using the Purpose-Driven Group Agreement. Healthy groups are alive. Conflict is a sign of maturity, not mistakes. Sometimes you may need to get outside counsel, but don't be afraid. See conflict as an opportunity to grow, and always confront it so it doesn't create a cancer that can kill the group over time (Matthew 18:15–20).

3. Lead from Weakness

The apostle Paul said that God's power was made perfect in Paul's weakness (2 Corinthians 12:9). This is clearly the opposite of what most leaders think, but it provides the most significant model of humility, authority, and spiritual power. It was Jesus' way at the cross. So share your struggles along with your successes, confess your sins to one another along with your celebrations, and ask for prayer for yourself along with praying for others. God will be pleased, and your group will grow deeper. If you humble yourself under God's mighty hand, he will exalt you at the proper time (Matthew 23:12).

4. What Makes Jesus Cry: A Leader's Focus

In Matthew 9:35–38, Jesus looked at the crowds following him and saw them as sheep without a shepherd. He was moved with compassion, because they were "distressed and downcast" (NASB); the NIV says they were "harassed and helpless." The Greek text implies that he was moved to the point of tears.

Never forget that you were once one of those sheep yourself. We urge you to keep yourself and your group focused not just inwardly to each other but also outwardly to people beyond your group. Jesus said, "Follow me . . . and I will make you fishers of men" (Matthew 4:19). We assume that you and your group are following him. So how is your fishing going? As leader, you can ignite in your group Jesus' compassion for outsiders. For his sake, keep the fire burning!

5. Prayer Triplets

Prayer triplets can provide a rich blessing to you and many others. At the beginning or end of your group meeting, you can gather people into prayer triplets to share and pray about three non-Christian friends. This single strategy will increase your group's evangelistic effectiveness considerably. Be sure to get an update on the plans and progress from each of the circles. You need only ten minutes at every other meeting—but do this at least once a month. At first, some of your members may feel overwhelmed at the thought of praying for non-Christians. We've been there! But you can be confident that over time they will be renewed in their heart for lost people and experience the blessing of giving birth to triplets.

6. Race against the Clock

When your group grows in size or your members begin to feel more comfortable talking, you will inevitably feel as though you're racing against the clock. You may know the feeling very well. The good news is that there are several simple things that can help your group stick to your agreed schedule:

- The time crunch is actually a sign of relational and spiritual health, so pat yourselves on the back.
- Check in with the group to problem-solve, because they feel the tension as well.

- You could begin your meeting a little early or ask for a later ending time.
- If you split up weekly into circles of three to four people for discussion, you will double the amount of time any one person can share.
- Appoint a timekeeper to keep the group on schedule.
- Remind everyone to give brief answers.
- Be selective in the number of questions you try to discuss.
- Finally, planning the time breaks in your booklet before the group meeting begins can really keep you on track.

7. All for One and One for All: Building a Leadership Team

The statement "Together Everybody Accomplishes More" (TEAM) is especially true in small groups. The Bible clearly teaches that every member is a minister. Be sure to empower the group to share weekly facilitation, as well as other responsibilities, and seek to move every player onto a team over time. Don't wait for people to ask, because it just won't happen. From the outset of your group, try to get everybody involved. The best way to get people in the game is to have the group suggest who would serve best on what team and in what role. See Purpose Team Roles on pages 70–71 for several practical suggestions. You could also talk to people individually or ask for volunteers in the group, but don't miss this opportunity to develop every group member and build a healthy and balanced group over time.

8. Purpose-Driven Groups Produce Purpose-Driven Lives: A Leader's Goal

As you undertake this new curriculum, especially if this is your first time as a leader, make sure you begin with the end in mind. You may have heard the phrase, "If you aim at nothing, you'll hit it every time." It's vital for your group members to review their spiritual health by using the Purpose-Driven Life Health Assessment and Purpose-Driven Life Health Plan (pages 72–76). You'll do part of the health assessment in your group in session 2 and share your results with spiritual partners for support and accountability. Each member will also set one goal for thirty days. The goal will be tied to the purpose you are studying in this particular guide. We strongly encourage you to go even further and do the entire health assessment together. Then during another group session (or on their own), members can set a goal for each of the other four purposes.

Pairing up with spiritual partners will offer invaluable support for that area of personal growth. Encourage partners to pray for one another in the area of their goals. Have partners gather at least three times during the series to share their progress and plans. This will give you and the group the best results. In order for people to follow through with their goals, you'll need to lead with vision and modeling. Share your goals with the group, and update them on how the steps you're taking have been affecting your spiritual life. If you share your progress and plans, others will follow in your footsteps.

9. Discover the Power of Pairs

The best resolutions get swept aside by busyness and forgetfulness, which is why it's important for group members to have support as they pursue a spiritual goal. Have them pair up with spiritual partners in session 2, or encourage them to seek out a Christian coworker or personal mentor. You can promise that they'll never be the same if they simply commit to supporting each other with prayer and encouragement on a weekly basis.

It's best to start with one goal in an area of greatest need. Most of the time the area will be either evangelism or consistent time with the Father in prayer and in Scripture reading. Cultivating time with God is the place to start; if group members are already doing this, they can move on to a second and third area of growth.

You just need a few victories in the beginning. Have spiritual partners check in together at the beginning or end of each group meeting. Ask them to support those check-ins with phone calls, coffee times, and E-mail messages during the week. Trust us on this one—you will see people grow like never before.

10. Don't Lose Heart: A Leader's Vision

You are a strategic player in the heavenly realm. Helping a few others grow in Christ could put you squarely in the sights of Satan himself. First Corinthians 15:58 (NASB) says, "Be steadfast, immovable, always abounding in the work of the Lord." Leading a group is not always going to be easy. Here are the keys to longevity and lasting joy as a leader:

- Be sure to refuel your soul as you give of yourself to others. We recommend that you ask a person to meet with you for personal coaching and encouragement. When asked (over coffee or lunch) to support someone in leadership, nine out of ten people say, "I'd love to!" So why not ask?
- Delegate responsibilities after the first meeting. Doing so will help group members grow, and it will give you a break as well.

- Most important, cultivating your own walk with God puts you on the offensive against Satan and increases the joy zone for everyone in your life. Make a renewed decision right now to make this happen. Don't give Satan a foothold in your heart; there is simply too much at stake.

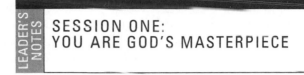

SESSION ONE:
YOU ARE GOD'S MASTERPIECE

Goals of the Session

- To realize that each of you is uniquely designed by God
- To understand that God wants to use your design for his good purposes

Open your meeting with a brief prayer.

Question 1. As leader, you should be the first to answer this question. Your answer will model the amount of time and vulnerability you want others to imitate. If you are brief, others will be brief. If your answer is superficial, you'll set a superficial tone—but if you tell something substantive and personal, others will know that your group is a safe place to tell the truth about themselves. You might want to think about your answer ahead of time.

Be sure to give each person a chance to respond to this question, because it's an opportunity for group members to get to know each other. It's not necessary to go around the circle in order. If certain persons have trouble thinking of something positive to say about themselves, allow for periods of silence. Don't jump in too quickly with a suggested answer, and restrain others from doing so. But if a person seems really stuck, you can offer your own observation about one of his or her positive qualities. Many people find it embarrassing to say anything good about themselves, as though it's bad luck or a sign of sinful pride. Some people genuinely believe that they have no good qualities. This study will provide many opportunities for the group to help them see themselves as the masterpieces they really are.

Introduction to the Series. If this is your first study guide in the DOING LIFE TOGETHER series, you'll need to take time after question 1 to orient the group to one principle that undergirds the series: *A healthy purpose-driven small group balances the five purposes of the church in order to help people balance them in their lives.* Most small groups emphasize Bible study, fellowship, and prayer. But God has called us to reach out to others as well. If the five purposes are new to your group, be sure to review the Read Me First section with your new group. In addition, the Frequently Asked Questions section could help your group understand some of the purpose-driven group basics.

Question 2. If your group has done another study guide in the DOING LIFE TOGETHER series within the past six months, you may not need to go over the Purpose-Driven Group Agreement again. It's a good idea to remind people of the agreement from time to time, but for an established group, recommitting every six months is reasonable. If you're new to the series and if you don't already have a group agreement, turn to page 67 and take about ten minutes to look at the Purpose-Driven Group Agreement. Read each value aloud in turn, and let group members comment at the end. Emphasize confidentiality—a commitment that is essential to the ability to trust each other.

"Spiritual Health" says that group members give permission to encourage each other to set spiritual goals *for themselves*. As the study progresses, a group member may set a goal to do daily devotions, or a dad may set a goal to spend half an hour each evening with his children. No one will set goals for someone else; each person will be free to set his or her own goals.

"Shared Ownership" points toward session 3, when members will be asked to help with some responsibility in the group. It may be as simple as bringing refreshments or keeping track of prayer requests. Ultimately, it's healthy for groups to rotate leadership among several, or perhaps even all, members. People grow when they contribute. However, no one should feel pressured into a responsibility.

Regarding expectations: It's amazing how many groups never take the time to make explicit plans about refreshments, child care, and other such issues. Child care is a big issue in many groups. It's important to treat it as an issue that the group as a whole needs to solve, even if the group decides that each member will make arrangements separately.

If you feel that your group needs to move on, you can save the conversation about expectations until the end of your meeting.

Question 3. Have someone read the Bible passage aloud. It's a good idea to ask someone ahead of time, because not everyone is comfortable reading aloud in public. When the passage has been read, ask question 3. Don't be afraid to allow silence while people think. It's completely normal to have periods of silence in a Bible study. You might count to seven silently. If nobody says anything, say something humorous like, "I can wait longer than you can!" It's not necessary that everyone respond to every one of the Bible study questions.

Question 4. People's thoughts may go to their worst sin or most dreadful experience of violation, and they may not want to share these things. Allow for some silence, and if no one steps up to share, you might offer a difficult experience of your own that seems appropriate for your group to hear. Maybe you have a physical ailment that limits what you can do for God.

Maybe you've been divorced, or you struggle with shyness, or you're not much of a Bible expert.

Question 9. If your group is brand-new, you may want to skip this exercise. But if you've been together for four sessions or more, people will know each other well enough to do this exercise. You will need to bring cards and pens to the meeting. You may be astonished at how highly people treasure this kind of card, as well as how blind some individuals can be to strengths that everyone else can see in them. People rarely get this kind of affirmation; don't miss the opportunity to give it to them.

Question 10. The devotional passages on page 81 give your group a chance to try out the spiritual discipline of spending daily time with God. Encourage everyone to give it a try. There are five short readings for each session, so people can read one a day and even skip a couple of days a week. Talk to your group about committing to reading and reflecting on these verses each day. This practice has revolutionized the spiritual lives of others who have used this study, so we highly recommend it. There will be an opportunity in future sessions to share what you have discovered in your devotional reading. Remind group members of the sample journal page on page 84.

Beginning in session 2, people will have an opportunity to check in with one other member at the end of several of the group sessions to share what they learned from the Lord in their devotional time.

Consider giving one or more group members the chance to be a facilitator for a meeting. Healthy groups rotate their leadership each week. No one person has to carry all the responsibility. What's more, it helps develop everyone's gifts in a safe environment, and, best of all, you learn different things through the eyes of different people with different styles. You can use the Small Group Calendar (page 69) to help manage your rotating schedule.

Question 11. Some groups really enjoy the chance to hear each person's prayer request in full detail. However, if your group is larger than six people, doing so can take considerable time. Smaller prayer circles give people more airtime to share their requests, as well as a less intimidating setting in which to take their first steps in praying aloud. If your group feels strongly about hearing everyone's requests, you can ask one person in each small circle to be the recorder and write down the requests. After the circles have finished praying, the recorder from each circle can briefly report the requests to the group. Members who want to hear the whole story can ask each other after the meeting.

You are the expert about your group. If your members are seasoned veterans in group prayer, let them go for it. But if you have members who are new believers, new to small groups, or just new to praying aloud, suggest an option that will feel comfortable for them. Newcomers won't come back if they find themselves in the scary position of having to pray aloud as "perfectly" as the veterans. Talking to God is more significant than talking to your nation's president or to a movie star—so it's no wonder people feel intimidated! A silent prayer, a one-sentence prayer, or even a one-word prayer are completely acceptable first steps. Make sure the circles understand this so that no one feels he or she is being put on the spot.

If you have an existing group, some group members may resist structural change—or any kind of change for that matter. Encourage them to test-drive the new format with an open mind, and see what God may do. You never know—it may generate fresh gusts of wind for the sails of your group.

SESSION TWO:
A SERVANT'S HEART

LEADER'S NOTES

Goals of the Session

- To understand what it means to have a true servant's heart
- To renew your commitment to serving others as Jesus did for us
- To set a goal for personal growth over the next thirty days

New rotating leaders may want to meet ahead of time with an experienced leader to review the plan for the meeting. You may want to have some extra booklets on hand for any new group members.

Questions 2–3. These questions set up a tension that everyone faces. We all want to feel valued, respected, and significant. God values and respects us, just the way a loving parent values and respects a child—*before we do anything*. We are significant to God just because he created us. We gain even more greatness in his kingdom by serving others, whether or not people are impressed. But the world values us if we make money, have an impressive job, become ministry leaders, have high-achieving children, and so on. We may not have time to do the things that impress the world *and* the things that warm God's heart. We often have to choose.

It's very important that people not see service as a to-do list of ministry accomplishments we carry out in order to impress God. If we are running a rat race of service in order to achieve greatness in God's eyes, we've missed the point. God values us before we do anything. Service is the restful heart's response to love, to being set free from the world's rat race.

Question 5. Jesus served us by dying to save our lives. He also served us by giving up the glory of heaven for a time in order to live as a human in circumstances we often associate with Third-World countries. If it would be a sacrifice for you to give up your current comforts to live in the most primitive conditions, imagine what it was like for Jesus to give up total intimacy with the Father. For thirty years Jesus experienced hunger, illness, cruelty—the full range of human suffering. His life as the teacher and model of a life well lived was just as much an act of service as his death.

Question 6. Paul's words conflict with much of today's conventional wisdom about taking care of yourself. He wasn't much concerned about a person's self-esteem or comfort. But it is helpful to read his words in context. Paul and

97

Jesus both willingly gave up their lives in order to spread the good news of God's love. This is the level of service to which you're called. Yet they avoided burnout. How? First, they weren't driven by ego (the need to impress people) or fear (the fear of disappointing people)—which helped them stay focused and say no to some requests. Every "no" was a "yes" to something more important. They lived with limits; they didn't try to do everything. Still, they were risk takers who spent their lives freely and didn't concern themselves with status.

Question 7. Jesus had a glorious, joyful, powerful life with the Father and the Holy Spirit before he set it all aside to become human for our sake. That's far more dramatic than a businessperson leaving a high-paying job to start a ministry for the poor—but even the businessperson's action would amaze us.

Question 10. Don't miss this opportunity to pray for each other while the needs are fresh in your minds. It's not necessary to pray only at the end of a meeting; you can do it whenever a need arises.

Question 11. Familiarize yourself with the Purpose-Driven Life Health Assessment before the meeting. You may want to take the assessment yourself ahead of time and think about your goal. Then you can give group members a real-life example of what you are actually committed to doing. We also encourage you to complete a simple goal under each purpose. Ask your coleader or a trusted friend to review it with you. Then you'll understand the power of this tool and the support you can gain from a spiritual partner.

Offer this health assessment in a spirit of grace. It should make people hungry to see the Holy Spirit work in their lives, not ashamed that they're falling short. Nobody can do these things in the power of the flesh! And sometimes the most mature believers have the clearest perception of the areas in which they need considerable help from the Spirit.

Question 12. Help guide group members to pair up with partners with whom they will have a good chemistry. Spiritual partnership works best when people trust each other. Point out the Spiritual Partners' Check-In Page on page 77, which can give partners a structure for checking in with each other. Bear in mind that some personalities love self-assessments and setting goals, while others are more resistant. Some people who routinely set goals at work may be taken aback at the idea of setting a goal for their spiritual lives. Assure everyone that their goals can be small steps, that no one will be pressured into performing or humiliated for falling short, and that God is always eager to give grace.

SESSION THREE: DISCOVERING YOUR GIFTS

Goals of the Session

- To understand that every believer has essential gifts and abilities to offer the body of Christ
- To become more aware of how God has gifted you
- To help others discern your gifts and abilities

Question 1. This is an opportunity for people to share in a lighthearted way their enthusiasm for or misgivings about the ticklish subject of spiritual gifts.

Question 2. If all gifts come from the same source, all believers are on the same level. Nobody's gift is more spiritual than someone else's. Gifts should be a source of unity, not division.

Question 4. The comparison to a human body helps us value each other's differences. No person can say he's not a real Christian because he doesn't have some particular gift. No person can say another Christian is unnecessary because she doesn't have some particular gift. Just as hands aren't better than feet, so a person with one design isn't better than a person with another design. Differences show that *we need each other* to get the work of the body done. Nobody can fulfill his or her purpose without the partnership of others.

Question 5. Beliefs about our inferiority can be deeply rooted in defining moments of our lives. Many people recall with profound pain the moment when they didn't get chosen for a baseball team or when a teacher told them they were stupid. It's not enough to mentally assent to the truth of 1 Corinthians 12. We need to let the truth of our high value sink deep into our hearts and dislodge the poisoned thorns of the past.

Questions 6–7. Allow about ten minutes for people to identify their gifts and abilities on their own.

Question 8. It will be helpful if the group takes five minutes for each group member. You can shorten the time per person if necessary, but be sure everyone gets some time for feedback from the group. It's very common for people to be blind to their own gifts but to see others' gifts clearly. Community is often the place where people best discover who they are. Please don't let just a few people dominate this exercise. If your time is limited, consider dividing into small circles of three or four people so that everyone can get feedback from at least a few people.

Goals of the Session

- To better understand and appreciate your own personality
- To better understand and appreciate the personalities of others in your group
- To commit to serving in your group in a way that fits you

Question 1. This is such a fun question that people can drag it out into a long discussion. Keep things moving. Group members should be able to answer in one minute each. If necessary, you can interrupt gently and put the group back on track.

Questions 2–3. Among other things, Paul was intense, smart, self-confident, and extremely zealous. These traits caused him to lead violent attacks on his enemies before he came to faith in Jesus Christ. After he came to faith, humility and nonviolence tempered him. He became able to channel his traits into boldness and an unflagging zeal to proclaim the gospel despite terrible opposition. Second Corinthians 11:16–29 describes some of the obstacles that Paul faced, which required boldness, intelligence, and determination.

Question 4. Mary had her own quiet kind of boldness and passion. Her voice was never heard in this story, but her actions spoke volumes as she defied social convention in order to express her love for Jesus and her grief at his coming death. Instead of serving the food, as women normally did (notice Martha), Mary spent money and her reputation wantonly in worship of her Lord. Instead of merely speaking her intuition that Jesus was going to die, she enacted it.

Question 5. Mary leads us to worship, not by her great preaching, but by her quiet and passionate example.

Question 7. This is a quick-and-dirty assessment; group members ought not to agonize over it. The important thing for each person is to gain some insight into himself or herself and each other. Understanding and appreciating each other's differences can help your group weather conflict productively, as people learn to work together instead of fighting over their different needs.

Question 10. This is an opportunity for members to begin to share ownership of the group. Some groups expect the leader to do everything, but healthy groups come to share responsibilities over time. By taking on small tasks like these, members will also discover and develop their gifts and interests with regard to serving others. Experimenting with acts of service will eventually help people identify how God has uniquely designed them for ministry. The suggested tasks are only ideas. Encourage group members to decide for themselves what would be good ways to serve the group. Ideally, get the group to go to the Purpose Team sheet (page 70). This will give a comprehensive understanding of the concept. You want to move forward with the presumption that each member will participate on a team or fill a role.

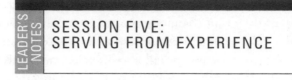

SESSION FIVE:
SERVING FROM EXPERIENCE

Goals of the Session

- To discover how your past experiences can be used to serve the Lord
- To share some of the experiences that have shaped who you are today

This session is designed to draw out a range of experiences that have equipped group members to serve God. Positive experiences are fairly easy to talk about and to link with present competence. It's relatively easy to see that someone with experience fixing cars might be able to help out in a ministry that provides free mechanic services to low-income families.

Painful experiences, however, are harder to talk about and harder to link with present potential. Many people have at least one past experience they see as hindering or disqualifying them from serving God. It may be a big sin they committed, a personal weakness, a time when they were sinned against, or a time when they feel that God let them down. The Bible passage in this session—the story of Peter denying that he knew Jesus—is an example of a sin that might make someone feel unworthy to serve. Other painful experiences include a history of promiscuity or physical abuse, or watching a loved one die. This session will be successful if group members come to see that God can use *everything* in their past to bring glory to him and to help others become more glorious. As leader, your central tasks in this session will be to help people (1) hear this theme in the Bible story and (2) share and hear their own and each other's hard stories. Sharing and being heard helps people embrace their painful experiences as the raw material for lives of valuable service.

This session, with its Bible study about Peter, won't be nearly as effective if people leave with only a head knowledge. God wants to reach their hearts. The discussion could be intense, and there may be tears. The group will feel safe allowing some intensity and emotion if you show that you welcome honest emotions and that you have everyone's needs in mind. Ideally, everyone should have a chance to share something in response to question 11, so you should keep the discussion moving in the event that one person tries to dominate the group's time and emotions. On the other hand, you'll want to be sensitive if someone's coming to grips with an experience really does require twenty minutes of the group's time. There are occasions when one person's need should become the group's priority. By this point in your group's life, you probably have a sense of which members consistently seek as much attention as possible (and thus can be gently asked to restrain themselves so that others can share) and which members don't ask for more time unless they really need it. In some cases it will be best to say, "This sounds really important. We need to let others share now, but may you and I talk more about this after the meeting?"

Questions 2–5. Before Jesus' arrest, Peter was arrogantly confident of his own ability to be courageous. He thought himself to be invincible. But when the moment of actual danger to his life came, he crumbled. In such a situation, it would be normal to feel humiliated, shocked, and disoriented. People with a lot of false pride can be vicious to themselves when they fail to live up to their own expectations. They are their own harshest critics. Jesus knew that Peter had feet of clay, but the reality may have been a terrifying shock to Peter.

Questions 6–8. Jesus knew he couldn't pretend that Peter's betrayal never happened. People don't grow from failure when failure is swept under the rug. Jesus came up with a wise way of letting Peter know both that Jesus took the betrayal seriously and that he forgave Peter completely. He allowed Peter to replace three denials of love with three affirmations of love. He handled the situation in a way that restored Peter's confidence without feeding his ego.

Question 9. Leaders who have faced and dealt with their own failures are less likely to be driven by ego in their dealings with the people they lead. Peter was less likely to have unreasonable expectations of himself or others and more likely to treat others' failures in the same serious but grace-filled way he was treated by Jesus. Humility is essential for the kind of compassion that truly feeds someone's soul.

SESSION SIX:
SERVING WITH YOUR
WHOLE HEART

Goals of the Session

- To discover an area of service you're passionate about
- To commit to an area of service

Questions 2–3. Paul says that God wants everyone to know a glorious secret (Colossians 1:27). Paul shares this desire. He's passionate about helping every person know Jesus Christ and come to maturity in Christ. He's willing to endure hard work, suffering, and even jail because his desire is so strong. Some people think that Christianity is about suppressing our desires. It's clear from Paul that Christianity is about having strong, clear, high desires for great things.

Question 4. A strong imagination for future glory was part of what fueled Paul's eagerness to serve in the present. Heaven isn't just insipid halos and harps. Get your imagination going. What future would be glorious enough to motivate you to pour yourself into the present? Consider these words of C. S. Lewis: "To please God . . . to be a real ingredient in the divine happiness . . . to be loved by God, not merely pitied, but delighted in as an artist delights in his work or a father in a son—it seems impossible, a weight or burden of glory which our thoughts can hardly sustain. But so it is." For more on Lewis's insightful reflections on glory, see his book *The Weight of Glory* (San Francisco: HarperSanFrancisco, first HarperCollins edition 2001).

Question 5. If Paul is an example of maturity, then maturity cannot be defined as "stiffly following all the rules." It's intense passion for and intimacy with Jesus Christ.

Question 6. Many people have no idea what it would be like to be as excited about something as Paul was. Give them permission to say so. People don't become fruitful servants for the long haul just because they should. A sense of duty is a good thing, but it's not enough unless it's a *passionate, wholehearted commitment* to an important duty. People become dry or burned out when they serve in order to feel okay about themselves or because they feel they have to. If your group members are resistant to service, they may simply not have learned to care. Some group members may be compulsive servants who have been going through the motions for years with deadness in their hearts. Spend some time talking about what could be missing in those who don't care.

Question 7. An accomplishment can be completing a school assignment, seeing one of your relationships restored, helping a friend, building something, playing music, creating art, competing in athletics—anything you accomplished that you enjoyed in the process. Don't choose something you did but would have been happy never to do again. Also, choose something you *accomplished*, not just something you enjoyed. Example: A summer at camp is not an accomplishment; finding a rare frog at summer camp is an accomplishment.

Question 10. It will be helpful if you take to this meeting a list of ministry opportunities in your church or community. People often need a menu to choose from. Some people will truly be in a season when they should say no to service. Some will already be serving; they just need to have this work acknowledged and affirmed. Others will be busy with tasks that are distractions from the service for which they were made. Take some time to help each other discern what God is calling each person to.

Question 12. This can take twenty minutes or more, but it's worth it. Don't worry about having the right words to say in a prayer. You can pray briefly for people if this kind of thing is new to you. You may be surprised to find what a profoundly moving experience it can be for your group members to have others lay hands on them and pray for them.

ABOUT THE AUTHORS

Brett and Dee Eastman have served at Saddleback Valley Community Church since July 1997, after previously serving for five years at Willow Creek Community Church in Illinois. Brett's primary responsibilities are in the areas of small groups, strategic planning, and leadership development. Brett has earned his Masters of Divinity degree from Talbot School of Theology and his Management Certificate from Kellogg School of Business at Northwestern University. Dee is the real hero in the family, who, after giving birth to Joshua and Breanna, gave birth to identical triplets—Meagan, Melody, and Michelle. Dee is the coleader of the women's Bible study at Saddleback Church called "The Journey." They live in Las Flores, California.

Todd and Denise Wendorff have served at Saddleback Valley Community Church since 1998. Todd is a pastor in the Maturity Department at Saddleback, and Denise coleads a women's Bible class with Dee Eastman called "The Journey." Todd earned a Masters of Theology degree from Talbot School of Theology. He has taught Biblical Studies courses at Biola University, Golden Gate Seminary, and other universities. Previously, Todd and Denise served at Willow Creek Community Church. They love to help others learn to dig into God's Word for themselves and experience biblical truths in their lives. Todd and Denise live in Trabuco Canyon, California, with their three children, Brooke, Brittany, and Brandon.

Karen Lee-Thorp has written or cowritten more than fifty books, workbooks, and Bible studies. Her books include *A Compact Guide to the Christian Life*, *How to Ask Great Questions*, and *Why Beauty Matters*. She was a senior editor at NavPress for many years and series editor for the LifeChange Bible study series. She is now a freelance writer living in Brea, California, with her husband, Greg Herr, and their daughters, Megan and Marissa.

SMALL GROUP ROSTER

Name	Address	Phone	E-mail Address	Team or Role	Church Ministry
Bill Jones	7 Alvalar Street L.F. 92665	766-2255	bjones@aol.com	socials	children's ministry

Be sure to pass your booklets around the room the first night, or have someone volunteer to type the group roster for all members. Encourage group ownership by having each member share a team role or responsibility.

Church Ministry	Team or Role	E-mail Address	Phone	Address	Name

Doing Life Together series

BRETT & DEE EASTMAN; KAREN LEE-THORP;
DENISE & TODD WENDORFF

Based on the five biblical purposes that form the bedrock of Saddleback Church, Doing Life Together will help your group discover what God created you for and how you can turn this dream into an everyday reality. Experience the transformation firsthand as you begin Connecting, Growing, Developing, Sharing, and Surrendering your life together for him.

"Doing Life Together is a groundbreaking study ... [It's] the first small group curriculum built completely on the purpose-driven paradigm ... The greatest reason I'm excited about [it] is that I've seen the dramatic changes it produces in the lives of those who study it."

— FROM THE FOREWORD BY RICK WARREN

Small Group Ministry Consultation

Building a healthy, vibrant, and growing small group ministry is challenging. That's why Brett Eastman and a team of certified coaches are offering small group ministry consultation. Join pastors and church leaders from around the country to discover new ways to launch and lead a healthy Purpose-Driven small group ministry in your church. To find out more information please call 1-800-467-1977.

Curriculum Kit	ISBN: 0-310-25002-1
Beginning Life Together	ISBN: 0-310-24672-5 Softcover
	ISBN: 0-310-25004-8 DVD
Connecting with God's Family	ISBN: 0-310-24673-3 Softcover
	ISBN: 0-310-25005-6 DVD
Growing to Be Like Christ	ISBN: 0-310-24674-1 Softcover
	ISBN: 0-310-25006-4 DVD
Developing Your SHAPE to Serve Others	ISBN: 0-310-24675-X Softcover
	ISBN: 0-310-25007-2 DVD
Sharing Your Life Mission Every Day	ISBN: 0-310-24676-8 Softcover
	ISBN: 0-310-25008-0 DVD
Surrendering Your Life for God's Pleasure	ISBN: 0-310-24677-6 Softcover
	ISBN: 0-310-25009-9 DVD

ZONDERVAN™

GRAND RAPIDS, MICHIGAN 49530 USA

WWW.ZONDERVAN.COM

lifetogether.com

The Purpose-Driven® Life
WHAT ON EARTH AM I HERE FOR?

RICK WARREN

The most basic question everyone faces in life is *Why am I here? What is my purpose?* Self-help books suggest that people should look within, at their own desires and dreams, but Rick Warren says the starting place must be with God — and his eternal purposes for each life. Real meaning and significance comes from understanding and fulfilling God's purposes for putting us on earth.

The Purpose-Driven Life takes the groundbreaking message of the award-winning *Purpose-Driven Church* and goes deeper, applying it to the lifestyle of individual Christians. This book helps readers understand God's incredible plan for their lives. Warren enables them to see "the big picture" of what life is all about and begin to live the life God created them to live.

The Purpose-Driven Life is a manifesto for Christian living in the 21st century — a lifestyle based on eternal purposes, not cultural values. Using biblical stories and letting the Bible speak for itself, Warren clearly explains God's 5 purposes for each of us:

We were planned for God's pleasure — experience real worship.
We were formed for God's family — enjoy real fellowship.
We were created to become like Christ — learn real discipleship.
We were shaped for serving God — practice real ministry.
We were made for a mission — live out real evangelism.

This long-anticipated book is the life-message of Rick Warren, founding pastor of Saddleback Church. Written in a captivating devotional style, the book is divided into 40 short chapters that can be read as a daily devotional, studied by small groups, and used by churches participating in the nationwide "40 Days of Purpose" campaign.

Hardcover: 0-310-20571-9   Unabridged Audio Pages® CD: 0-310-24788-8
Unabridged Audio Pages® cassette: 0-310-20907-2

Also available from Inspirio, the gift division of Zondervan

Purpose-Driven Life Journal: 0-310-80306-3
Planned for God's Pleasure (Gift Book):   0-310-80322-5
ScriptureKeeper® Plus Purpose-Driven® Life: 0-310-80323-3

We want to hear from you. Please send your comments about this book to us in care of the address below. Thank you.

ZONDERVAN™

GRAND RAPIDS, MICHIGAN 49530 USA

WWW.ZONDERVAN.COM